PLANTS & GARDE

BROOKLYN BOTANIC GARDEN RECORD

GARDENER'S WORLD OF
BULBS

1991

Brooklyn Botanic Garden

STAFF FOR THIS EDITION:

JUDY GLATTSTEIN, GUEST EDITOR

BARBARA B. PESCH, DIRECTOR OF PUBLICATIONS

JANET MARINELLI, ASSOCIATE EDITOR

AND THE EDITORIAL COMMITTEE OF THE BROOKLYN BOTANIC GARDEN

BEKKA LINDSTROM, ART DIRECTOR

JUDITH D. ZUK, PRESIDENT, BROOKLYN BOTANIC GARDEN

ELIZABETH SCHOLTZ, DIRECTOR EMERITUS, BROOKLYN BOTANIC GARDEN

STEPHEN K-M. TIM, VICE PRESIDENT, SCIENCE & PUBLICATIONS

COVER PHOTOGRAPH BY ELVIN MCDONALD

ILLUSTRATIONS BY RUTH SOFFER

Plants & Gardens, Brooklyn Botanic Garden Record (ISSN 0362-5850) is published quarterly at 1000 Washington Ave., Brooklyn, N.Y. 11225, by the Brooklyn Botanic Garden, Inc. Second-class-postage paid at Brooklyn, N.Y., and at additional mailing offices. Subscription included in Botanic Garden membership dues ($25.00) per year.

ISBN # 0-945352-62-X

PLANTS & GARDENS

BROOKLYN BOTANIC GARDEN RECORD

GARDENER'S WORLD OF BULBS

VOL. 47, NO. 2, SUMMER 1991

HANDBOOK #127

4

FOREWORD

Store displays of bulbs in autumn or spring give little hint of the peacock array of flowers waiting to delight us. Concealed beneath their plain brown wrappers, bulbs are almost magical, rarely failing to awaken the childlike sense of wonder in even the most experienced gardener.

Bulbs are a fascinating category of perennial plants. Their lumpy underground structure is designed to get them through hard times, whether winter cold or summer drought. It also makes them relatively easy to ship to market and plant in the garden. And what a diverse category of plants: There are bulbs for shady woodlands and sunny open areas, regions with mild winters and those with cold ones, locations with limited rainfall and others where precipitation is more abundant. Not all bulbs are winter hardy, or able to flower where winters are warm. But that doesn't stop dedicated gardeners, as many bulbs can be stored over harsh winters, refrigerated or grown in containers.

Bulbs are appropriate for the most formal herbaceous border or the most casual naturalistic garden. They can be massed for display in a public or private garden, or a small number can be used to enhance a mixed planting of perennials or native plants. They enchant us as the first flowers of spring, enlarge the sumptuous splendors of summer, provide the last blooms of autumn. There is a bulb for anyone who enjoys the pleasures of the garden, wherever the garden.

JUDY GLATTSTEIN
GUEST EDITOR

5

THE BOTANY OF BULBS

BY MOBEE WEINSTEIN

Definitions

Many people are familiar with tulips, daffodils and other bulbous plants. But what, exactly, are bulbs? Horticulturally speaking, the term "bulb" is often used loosely and refers not only to true bulbs but also to corms, tubers, rhizomes and tuberous roots. Although technically different, they all have one thing in common: They are highly specialized storage organs. Surviving adverse seasons of drought and/or extreme heat or cold underground, these food storage organs enable the plants to grow rapidly during favorable conditions.

Botanically speaking, a true bulb is a usually subterranean modified stem with leaves, complete with flowers in embryonic form. This can be seen by slicing through the bulb vertically. Bulbs consist of a basal plate from which the roots will grow and a thick, shortened stem surrounded by fleshy scale leaves. These scales contain the food necessary to sustain the bulb during dormancy and early growth. The basal plate also serves to hold these scales together. There are two types of bulbs:

tunicate and imbricate (sometimes referred to as scaly.) Tunicate bulbs have scales which are tightly wrapped around the bud and covered in a thin, dry papery skin called a tunic. *Tulipa, Narcissus* and *Hyacinthus* are examples. Imbricate bulbs have thick scales which are loosely arranged and may have no covering. An example is *Lilium,* the true lily.

During the growing season, small new bulbs, called bulblets, are produced from lateral buds on the basal plate. Some types, such as lilies, can also produce small bulbs, called bulbils, above ground in the axils of their leaves.

A corm is a modified stem also usually subterranean. The base of the stem becomes swollen and forms a solid mass of storage tissue. Like the true bulb, it has a basal plate from which the roots will grow. The corm has no fleshy scales, but is covered by dried leaf bases that resemble the tunic seen in many true bulbs. On the top of the corm you will find one or more growing points, or "eyes," from which the top growth will come. During the growing cycle, the corm is depleted of food reserves and is replaced by a new corm formed from buds on top of or beside the old one. In addition, some form small new corms,

MOBEE WEINSTEIN *is Assistant Foreman of Gardeners at New York Botanical Garden.*

called cormels or cormlets, around the basal plate. *Crocus, Gladiolus* and *Freesia* are all examples of corms.

Like the corm, a tuber is a modified stem which is usually subterranean. However, that is where the similarity ends. Tubers have no basal plate, nor do they have a tuniclike covering. They are usually swollen with food reserves and have growth buds, or eyes, scattered over the surface. Both roots and shoots emerge from these eyes. Some tubers, such as the potato and *Caladium,* diminish in size during the growing season, but produce new tubers from the buds of the original one. Others, like the tuberous begonia, gloxinia and *Cyclamen,* increase in size as they store food and produce new growth buds for the next season.

In addition to tubers and corms, rhizomes are modified stems too. Sometimes referred to as a rootstock, a rhizome is a thickened stem growing horizontally, usually below the soil surface. Roots grow from the lower surface, while shoots will develop from buds or eyes on the upper surface or sides, usually at the tip. *Canna,* certain types of *Iris* and the calla lily are all rhizomatous. Some plants like the lily-of-the-valley will send up detachable "pips" which are small, upright shoots with their own roots.

Different from all the others, tuberous roots are formed from root tissue. These swollen roots are modified specifically to store food. During the growing season, other fibrous roots are responsible for the uptake of water and nutrients. Occasionally, the growth buds, or eyes, are scattered over its surface, as in the sweet potato, but in most cases, these buds are restricted to that part of the old stem which joins with the tuberous root. This area is often called the crown. The *Dahlia* is an

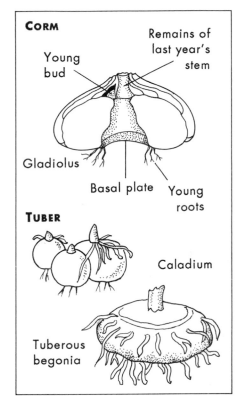

example of this type of storage organ.

From here on, I will use the term "bulb" in its broad sense, to include all five types of storage organs just described.

Distribution

Bulbs enjoy, for the most part, a worldwide distribution. Most regions of the world, with their varying environments and climates, offer representatives of this large and diverse group of plants.

The majority of our winter-hardy bulbs that can survive cold temperatures come from the Mediterranean region. This climate is characterized by cool, wet winters and hot, dry summers, often with a short

7

spring season. Although four other areas of the world have this type of climate, portions of California in North America, southern Chile in South America, the southern tip of Africa and the southern and western parts of Australia, they are not responsible for providing us with many hardy bulbs. A few very popular examples from the Mediterranean region are *Narcissus, Crocus, Muscari* and *Hyacinthus*. A number of other winter-hardy bulbs come from Asia and North America where the climate is considered temperate, having warm summers and cold winters. The highly favored *Tulipa,* many species of *Lilium,* and *Lycoris* all come from parts of Asia, while North America provides other species of *Lilium,* some species of *Fritillaria* and *Anemone,* as well as *Iris cristata.*

Although South Africa does not give us hardy bulbs, it is very rich in subtropical ones. These plants prefer cool growing conditions, but cannot tolerate freezing temperatures. As they are from the southern hemisphere, their seasons are opposite ours, and most of them are active in our fall and winter. Many garden favorites originate here: *Gladiolus, Freesia, Amaryllis, Clivia, Nerine* and *Agapanthus,* to name a few.

Geographically, the tropical zone reaches from the equator north to the Tropic of Cancer and south to the Tropic of Capricorn. Here, day length is consistent throughout the year. Outside of day length, these areas are not all similar. Due to other factors, such as the presence of bodies of water, ocean currents, the presence of mountains and their orientation and elevation, and atmospheric currents, the climatic zones do not follow precisely the geographic lines, nor do all the areas that fall within this belt share the same climatic conditions. Some regions of the tropics, in particular the tropical rain forests, have great amounts of annual precipitation which is evenly distributed throughout the year, as well as relatively warm, constant temperatures. Here, life is richest as the factors controlling growth are not limited. Other tropical areas may have seasonal dry periods, and still others experience very limited rainfall in conjunction with extreme temperatures and often tremendous daily fluctuations. As in other parts of the world, there are also zonal changes as you ascend mountains and the altitude increases. From the vast tropics of Africa, Asia and South America come many "bulbous" plants. *Alstroemeria, Dahlia, Caladium* and tuberous begonias all hail from South America. All species of *Alocasia* and *Colocasia* come from tropical Asia, while different species of *Crinum* come from all three regions. *Gloriosa* and *Acidanthera* come from tropical Africa.

Taxonomy and Nomenclature

As the horticultural and botanical definitions of the word bulb are different, so too are there differences between horticultural "families" of plants and botanical ones. Horticultural "families" are often based on certain gross similarities such as cultural requirements or their habit of growth — for example bulbs, vines or succulents. As with the term bulb, the horticultural usage is of a broader, more general scope than the botanical one.

Taxonomy is the science of classifying things into various categories or groups. Here we are concerned with the classification of plants. The first and largest category is called the kingdom and the subordinate categories become increasingly more specific in defining the boundaries of their members. More than one system of classification exists reflecting various differences in opinion. The characters that form the basis of distinction are diverse but usually

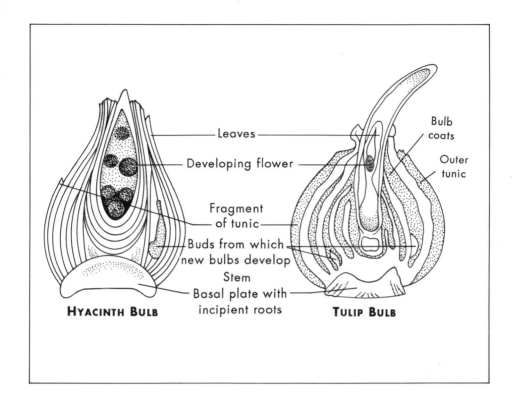

Leaves

Developing flower

Fragment of tunic

Buds from which new bulbs develop

Stem

Basal plate with incipient roots

Bulb coats

Outer tunic

HYACINTH BULB

TULIP BULB

are combinations of morphological features, particularly reproductive structures such as flowers and fruit. For our purposes, we will only concern ourselves with the category of the family and its subordinate groups. A family is composed of plants sharing certain characteristics but differing in others. It is further broken down into units known as genera, which in turn are separated into one or more species.

All plants are given botanical names composed of two parts according to the binomial system which was applied by Carolus Linnaeus, the founder of modern plant classification. The first part is called the genus (plural genera) and the second is referred to as the specific epithet. A species is referred to using both the genus and species epithet.

Botanical names are governed by the rules set forth by the International Code of Botanical Nomenclature. The genus is always written with a capital first letter. Both genus and species are italicized.

All in all, there are approximately three thousand species of bulbs in existence today and it is interesting to note that the majority of them come from only three families: the amaryllis family (Amaryllidaceae), the iris family (Iridaceae) and the lily family (Liliaceae).

This should serve as an introduction to the world of bulbs. A better understanding of the various types of storage organs and their growth patterns, as well as the varying conditions in which they grow, will help you cultivate these fascinating plants successfully.   ※

THE HISTORY OF
THE TULIP

BY CARLA TEUNE

In 1561 Conrad Gesner made an engraving of a tulip for the book of a friend, Valerius Cordus. The famous *Dodonaeus* (1568) included a picture of a tulip. However, it was Carolus Clusius (Charles d'Ecluse, born in 1526 in Utrecht) who received some bulbs (or possibly seeds) from Constantinople from his friend the Ambassador De Busbecq during a visit to Prague. In October 1593 Clusius became director (Horti Praefectus) of the Leiden University Hortus Medicus, which was planted under his supervision in 1594. We are more or less certain that Clusius grew in the Leiden Hortus a red and yellow tulip 'Zomerschoon' (Summer Beauty) in the spring of 1595. Although Clusius wasn't willing to part with these extremely rare beauties (he kept them in a special, enclosed part of the garden devoted to scientific research), unannounced "visitors" climbed over the rather low fence and stole some of the precious bulbs.

The tulip was so rare that only very rich noblemen and people in high government office in the two provinces of Holland could afford to buy the bulbs

---

CARLA TEUNE *is curator of the University Botanic Garden, Leiden, the Netherlands.*

in those first years. It wasn't until the early 17th century that Amsterdam merchants established the tulip trade, and even then, prices soared sky high. Records show that the variety 'Semper Augustus' (with white and red flamed or broken flowers) was sold in 1623 at the astounding price of 1000 Dutch guilders *for one bulb*. Two years later, two bulbs of the same variety fetched an offer of 3000 Dutch guilders; as this was considered far too low, the offer was rejected.

Fashion and status also kept prices high. For instance, among the High Society in Paris it became the height of fashion to adorn low-cut ladies' dresses with fresh-cut tulips. Tulips became the supreme status symbol as women vied for the rarest — and most expensive — tulips to display on their bosoms.

"Tulipomania," as we now call this period, began around 1634. According to an invoice, one bulb of the tulip 'Viceroy' was sold for:

2 cartloads of wheat
4 cartloads of rye
4 fat oxen
5 pigs
4 tubs of ale

Frontispiece from Carolus Clusius' *Rariorum Plantarum Historia*, 1601.

2 hogshead of wine
2 tubs of butter
a thousand pounds of cheese
one bed
some clothes
a silver beaker

All this was worth a total of about 2500 Dutch guilders, plus 500 more for a ship to transport it.

The most beloved tulips were the flamed, striped or broken varieties. In those days, people didn't understand how

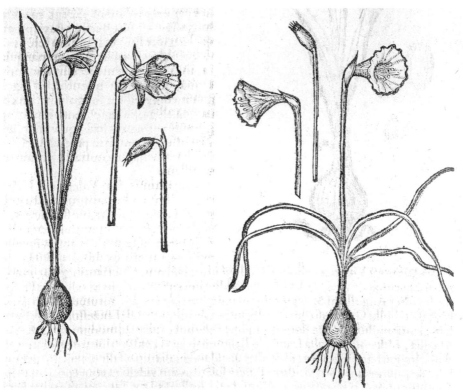

An early-17th century illustration of *Narcissus bulbocodium*, a name provided the hoop-petticoat daffodil by Linnaeus.

these broken flowers were possible. Today, of course, we know that they are the result of a virus easily transmitted from one plant to another by insects.

The tulips of the 1630s were rarely paid for in currency, but rather with certificates that promised a great deal but in reality were worthless — like some "junk bonds" today. Even the certificates themselves were traded. Inevitably, this rampant speculation ended in a big crash, which took place at an auction on the 3rd of February, 1637. It was the beginning of the end of tulipomania. The government of the two provinces of Holland took strict measures to prevent this kind of speculation from ever happening again. Many people were

financially ruined and forced to find new employment and start a new life. Only the innkeepers at whose establishments tulip speculators had gathered and traded made out well in the end.

The tulip Clusius received from Constantinople was not a wild species tulip but rather a cultivated plant. (Europe has its own wild tulips — *Tulipa sylvestris* and *T. grengiolensis*, for example. Tulips are also native to the area from Asia Minor and Iran through Asiatic Russia and western China.) Even in Turkey in those days a beautiful tulip fetched a good price. During the Ottoman Empire under Sultan Suleiman I (1494-1566) the tulip was a favorite flower. But it reached its pinnacle of popularity

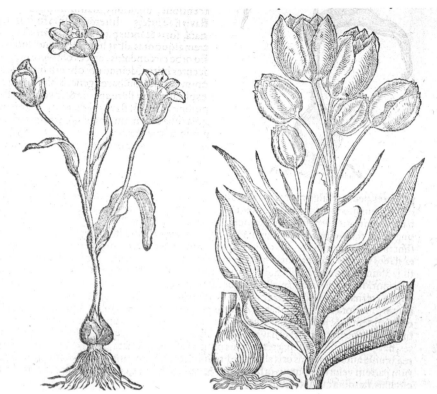

Tulipa serotina distinguished as *minor*, left, and *major*, right, in the 17th century.

under Sultan Ahmed III (1703-1730). He even imported tulips from Holland — he was curious to see what these foreigners had done with his beloved flower for the past 150 years. During this period, it was forbidden to take tulips out of Constantinople. Punishment was severe, and foreign visitors were warned that a man's life was far less valuable than a beautiful tulip. No wonder that in Constantinople this period is known as the Tulip Century!

The Turks kept a very strict register in which all existing and new tulips were described — over 1588 names are mentioned in this book, called *Ferahengiz*. In those days, the perfect flower was considered one which had petals in the shape of a needle or dagger. The petals had to touch, the three inner petals had to be smaller than the three on the outside and they had to cover the anthers and pistil entirely. What's more, the flower had to stand upright. All other flowers were considered worthless.

Although tulipomania ended in disaster for many people, it obviously was not the end of tulip cultivation in Holland. For a long time tulips (and other bulbs like hyacinths, daffodils, crocus and crown imperials) were grown primarily in the region between Leiden and Haarlem. The soil in this region was considered particularly good for bulb growing: light, sandy, well drained.

13

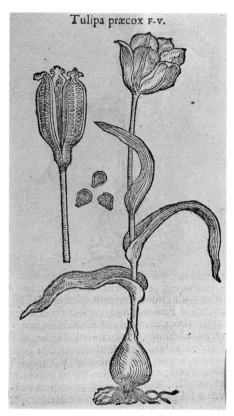

Tulipa præcox F-V.

Tulipa praecox.

Holland had approximately 13,000 bulb-growing firms; this number had dropped to 4,000 by 1988.

At the end of the 17th century bulbs were already exported to several countries, but for a very long time prices were high, and bulbs remained status symbols. Today bulbs are exported to more than 100 countries. In March, 1849, one Mr. van der Schoot, who lived in the bulb village of Sassenheim, left Holland by boat to try his luck as a bulb exporter in the U.S. In 1987 the United States took second place in the long list of countries that import Dutch bulbs; only Germany imported more. In 1989 Holland exported 4.3 billion bulbs, and more tulips were exported than any other bulb. Bulb exports grew that year by 5 percent. Tulip exports grew by 6 percent after a decline in the mid-eighties.

Much attention is paid to maintaining the quality of bulbs for export. Research continues on virus-free bulbs, pest control (especially non-chemical controls) and new propagation methods.

For 130 years the Dutch Bulb Growers Association (Koninklijke Algemeene Vereeniging voor Bloembollencultuur) has looked after the interests of some 4200 members. The association publishes a weekly bulletin in which new developments are described and bulb shows are announced. Every Monday members can meet at the association's headquarters in Hillegom to exchange tips on cultivating bulbs and see results of scientific research. And there are always bulbs to be judged.

The Dutch Bulb Growers Association has branch offices in several countries, including one in New York City. Every year huge shipments of bulbs are presented to cities and countries abroad, so that people around the world can experience the delight of Dutch tulips.

Nowadays, this area is still very important and known as the "Bollenstreek" or bulb area, but bulb growers have moved on to other parts of the country as well: North of Haarlem, around the villages of Limmen and Anna Paulowna and Breezand and even in the newly made polders in the old Zuiderzee, daffodil bulbs are grown today.

In recent decades, the acreage devoted to bulb growing has grown dramatically. In 1960 10,000 hectares were cultivated with bulbs; in 1989, more than 16,000 hectares. On the other hand, the number of bulb firms has decreased precipitously. In 1960

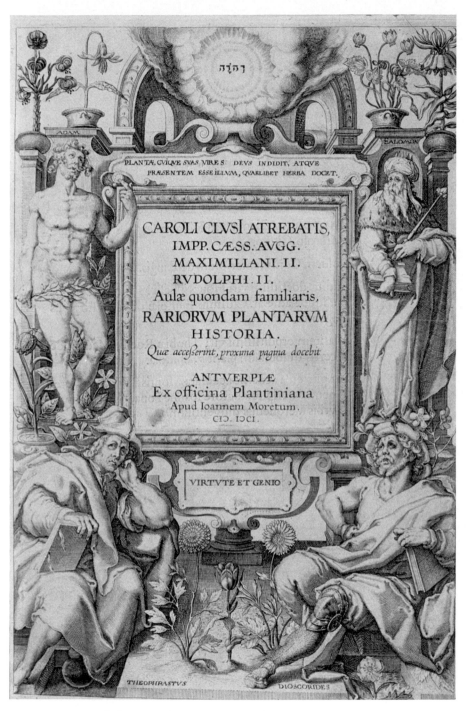

Title page from *Rariorum Plantarum Historia*.

Anemonella thalictroides.

PHOTOS BY AUTHOR

NATIVE AMERICAN BULBS FOR THE GARDEN

BY CHARLES COLSTON BURRELL

A prophet is seldom recognized in his or her native land. Nor, I am afraid, is a good bulb. In our quest for the unusual, we often overlook the obvious. The native flora of eastern North America contains a great diversity of easily cultivated garden-worthy plants. From woodlands, fields and prairies come a dozen showy genera that have a place in every garden. A little extra attention to soil and moisture conditions gains experienced gardeners a few extra species whose

CHARLES COLSTON BURRELL *is a garden designer, freelance garden writer and photographer. His design business, Native Landscapes, specializes in landscape restoration and in the innovative use of native plants and perennials. He is the author of* Perennial Portraits, 1991, *a calendar of outstanding perennial plants.*

Claytonia.

beauty repays the extra effort ten-fold.

Many native spring-flowering bulbs are referred to as "spring ephemerals." Like traditional garden denizens such as crocus and narcissus, the plants use the energy stored within their bulbs to put on a quick spurt of growth in early spring. They flower, set seed and disappear before the forest canopy closes in, blocking the sunlight for the remainder of the season. Once they're dormant, the soil in which they grow can be allowed to become quite dry without detrimental effects, although moisture is preferable.

Summer-flowering species, and certain of the non-ephemeral spring bloomers, require even moisture throughout the growing season. The later blooming species invariably require some direct sunlight and many will thrive in full sun.

Alliums (wild onions) are excellent summer-blooming bulbs for full to partial sun. Their starry six-petaled flowers are borne in rounded clusters atop slender stems. *Allium cernuum*, the nodding onion, is a large plant to two feet with flattened, gray-green foliage and dense umbels of white, pink or rose flowers that open from nodding buds. *Allium stellatum*, starry onion, a

prairie native, is more delicate, with smaller umbels of rose-pink flowers on one-foot stalks. *Allium tricoccum*, wild leek, prefers open woods and blooms after the showy spring leaves have disappeared. The cream to greenish flowers are often overlooked in the shaded summer woodland. Alliums are best propagated from seed or by dividing the tightly packed bulbs in spring or fall.

Anemonella (Thalictrum) thalictroides, rue anemone, is a dainty woodland denizen with airy foliage and white to rose flowers that seem too large to be supported by their four-to-nine-inch threadlike stems. The plant blooms tirelessly throughout the spring and disappears altogether by midsummer. The delicate tuberous roots are easily divided in summer or fall, or you can sow fresh seed in outdoor beds.

The genus *Arisaema* contains two species that are of interest to gardeners for their attractive foliage and intriguing floral structures. The petals are replaced by a fleshy hood called a spathe, similar to that of a calla lily, which surrounds a central reproductive column called a spadix. *Arisaema triphyllum*, jack-in-the-pulpit, has single or paired leaves with three broad

Camassia scilloides.

leaflets borne on a fleshy stalk to three feet. The showy green spathe, produced in April and May, is striped with purple, brown or light green. *Arisaema dracontium*, green dragon, has a single leaf with seven to fifteen leaflets arranged in a semi-circle around the central stalk. The long, awl-like spadix protrudes majestically from an inconspicuous green spathe. Mature plants may reach four feet in height with a two-foot spread. Jack-in-the-pulpit requires moist, humus-rich soil in sun or deep shade. Green dragon needs moist to wet soil, will not tolerate drying out and prefers full to partial sun. Arisaemas are excellent accent plants and the persistent foliage is useful in the summer garden. Both species have showy, orange-red fruits that should be cleaned from their pulp and sown outdoors when ripe or indoors with six weeks of cold, moist stratification. (Stratification is the practice of placing seeds between layers of moist sand or peat and exposing them to low temperatures. The treatment is necessary for seeds that require a period of chilling before they will germinate.). Tubers should be transplanted while dormant.

Amianthium muscaetoxicum, fly poison, is a handsome native of acidic woodlands and savannas of the southeastern U.S. The bulb produces a mound of attractive strap-like foliage and a single two-foot flowering stalk bearing a dense, elongate cluster of creamy white flowers that fade to green. Somewhat finicky, the plants like humus-rich, sandy soil that is moist but well drained. Propagate by sowing seed outdoors when ripe or indoors with warm moist, then cold moist stratification. Bulbs can be divided when dormant.

Camassia scilloides, wild hyacinth, is a lovely denizen of low meadows and wet woods of the eastern U.S. The pale blue, starry flowers are produced in open, elongate clusters on one-to-two-foot stalks. Tricky to cultivate, the plant requires constant moisture, cool rich soil and full sun. In warmer areas, provide afternoon shade and a cool root run. Plants go dormant after flowering and can be allowed to dry out. Two western species with pale to vibrant blue flowers, *Camassia leichtlinii* and *C. quamash,* are of easy culture, but are not often grown outside their native ranges. Propagate by division when dormant. Seeds germinate readily with cold, moist stratification but require

Lilium superbum.

many years to flower.

Claytonias, the spring beauties, are spring ephemerals that produce a wealth of foliage and flowers from small corms. The first leaves emerge in earliest spring, closely followed by the delicate white or pale rose-pink flowers. After four weeks of nonstop bloom, the plants disappear as quickly as they emerged. The plants make charming carpets among shrubs, in the lawn, or with other woodland plants. *C. virginica* has grass-like leaves while those of *C. caroliniana* are oval to broadly lanceolate. They thrive in moist, rich to average soil. Summer drought will not harm the dormant corms. Propagate by sowing fresh seed outdoors or by dividing the corm with a sharp knife after flowering.

Dentaria, also listed as *Cardamine*, is a genus of ephemeral woodland species that perform well in the spring shade garden. *Dentaria laciniata*, toothwort, has three

Allium stellatum.

Lilium philadelphicum.

Lilium michiganense.

Lilium columbianum.

ragged, palmate leaves in a whorl below an open cluster of nodding pale pink flowers. *D. diphylla*, crinkleroot, has broad, thrice-divided basal leaves and six-to-eight-inch flowering stalks bearing paired leaves and flower clusters as above. Dentarias grow from brittle rhizomes that creep at or just below the surface in moist, loamy or humus-rich soils. Propagate by careful division of the dormant rhizome or by fresh seed sown outdoors.

Dicentras grow from fragile bulblet-bearing rootstocks. They are ephemeral woodland denizens that produce mounds of ferny foliage and nodding white flowers. *Dicentra cucullaria*, dutchman's breeches, bears a string of inverted pantaloons on eight-to-ten-inch stalks. The smaller squirrel corn, *D. canadensis*, has a cluster of heart-shaped flowers scented like hyacinths. These natives of rocky woods

Erythronium montanum.

21

Zephyranthes atamasco.

and riverbanks thrive in moist, humusy soil. They are dormant by June, so the soil can become quite dry with no ill effects. Use dicentras to accent taller plants such as bellworts and trilliums, or as a carpet with ferns that will fill in when the foliage disappears. Protection from rodents is advisable. Propagate by sowing fresh seed outdoors or by division of the bulblets.

The erythroniums or trout lilies are dainty spring wildflowers of exceptional beauty. They form large patches of brown-mottled foliage above which the open bell-shaped flowers nod on delicate stems. *Erythronium americanum* has yellow flowers while those of *E. albidum* are white with a blush of violet. They grow best in rich, moist woodland soil. Plants spread by underground stolons to form dense colonies that may get too thick to flower well. Several western species, including *Erythronium californicum* (creamy white), *E. grandiflorum* (yellow), *E. hendersonii* (purple) and *E. revolutum* (white to rose) are worth investigating. They do best in partial shade with cool, moist soil. Propagate from fresh seed or by dividing dormant clumps.

Fritillaria is a western genus that is seldom grown in the East. The most dependable species is *F. lanceolata*, mission bells, which has brown-purple rounded bells mottled with green. *F. biflora* (brown) and *F. pudica* (yellow) are also worth trying. They require rich, well-drained soil and should be protected from drying winds and hot afternoon sun. Plants should be left undisturbed once established.

Hymenocallis occidentalis, spider lily, and *Crinum americanum*, swamp lily, are two bulbs from the coastal Southeast that grow in low woods and pine savannas. The large bulbs produce mounds of coarse, linear foliage. In spring and summer a stout stem produces stunning white flowers that distinguish these two similar plants. Spider lily has thin straplike petals and a central saucer-shaped membrane that overlays the petals. Swamp lily flowers have six narrow, recurved to flat petals but lack the connecting membrane. Flowers of both are fragrant. Plant the bulbs in moist, rich, acid soil, in full sun or light shade. Propagate by separating offsets or dividing overgrown clumps while they are dormant. Fresh seed can be sown indoors or out.

Hypoxis hirsuta, gold stargrass, is a diminutive bulb that blooms all season. The narrow, grassy foliage seldom reaches

Erythronium americanum.

a foot in height and the flower stalk is usually much shorter. The three-quarter-inch yellow flowers are indeed starlike and are borne in loose clusters. Hypoxis grows in sandy, acid woodlands as well as on calcareous prairies. In the garden, give it moist, well-drained sandy soil. Propagation is best accomplished by dividing the corms during the fall or early spring.

The genus *Lilium* is well represented in the flora of the eastern and central states. *L. philadelphicum* is the most widespread, from the Great Plains to New England and South. Its scarlet to orange flowers are distinctive, upward-facing cups. *L. superbum, L. michauxii* and *L. michiganense* are similar to one another, with spotted, red-orange to orange flowers with strongly reflexed petals. *L. canadense* has yellow to red nodding bells. Native lilies require cool, rich soil with even moisture. They like their feet in the shade and their heads in the sun. *L. philadelphicum* prefers sandy acid soils and is more heat tolerant. Lilies have become increasingly rare in the wild and, like all native plants, should never be collected. Purchase only from reputable dealers known to propagate their stock, or grow your own from fresh seed sown outdoors.

Seed can be sown indoors by giving a warm moist, then a cold moist stratification before growing the seedlings on. They may take five or more years to flower. Scaling the bulbs is also effective (removing a few firm scales from the outside of the bulbs for propagation); young plants will flower in three years. They must be protected from rodents.

Stenanthium gramineum, feather-fleece, is a robust, late summer bloomer with a two-to-five-foot, airy cluster of creamy white flowers. The plants require rich, highly acid soils in full sun for best growth. The grasslike foliage is attractive from spring onward. Propagate by dividing the bulbs when dormant.

Trilliums are the most sought after of the bulbous natives and are all too often collected from the wild. Few dealers are propagating the plants they sell. Do not buy trilliums unless you are positive the plants are propagated. One or more stout stalks rise from what is actually a rhizome and bear three, broadly oval leaves in a whorl. The single flower has three showy petals and three conspicuous petals. There are two groups, the stalked and the sessile trilliums. They differ in that sessile trilliums have

Fritillaria lanceolata.

mottled leaves and bear their flowers directly from the whorl of foliage while the others have erect or nodding stalks that hold the flowers. *Trillium grandiflorum* is the showiest, with large white petals that fade to rose. *T. erectum* varies from blood red to yellow and cream. *T. vaseyi* is similar with larger flowers. *T. stylosum* has slightly nodding, pale pink flowers, while *T. cernuum* and *T. flexipes* hide their white flowers below the foliage. *T. undulatum* is striking, with white petals dashed with crimson at their bases. The diminutive *T. nivale* is the first to bloom, often before the snow is melted. Of the sessile forms, *T. cuneatum* (maroon), *T. luteum* (yellow), *T. discolor* (pale yellow), and *T. recurvatum* (purple-brown) are recommended. Of the western species, *T. ovatum* (white) is the showiest. *T. chloropetalum* is a purple sessile type.

Trilliums thrive in evenly moist, humus-rich soils but are widely tolerant of condi-

Arisaema triphyllum.

Dicentra cucullaria.

24

Trillium nivale.

Trillium flexipes.

tions under cultivation. *T. nivale* must have near neutral soil and *T. undulatum* requires cool, highly acidic humus. Trilliums are easily propagated from fresh seed sown outdoors but may take up to seven years to bloom. The sessile species bloom in three to five years. Clumps can be divided when dormant and nicking the rhizome will produce offsets.

Zephyranthes atamasco, atamasco lily, is a small, spring-flowering bulb to one foot of wet open woods and pine savannas. The gorgeous four-inch white flowers open from slender buds as the straplike leaves are emerging. Atamasco requires moist to wet, sandy, acid soil in full sun. Plants languish in shade and never bloom. Propagate from seed sown fresh outdoors, or provide six weeks of cold moist stratification indoors. Divide the bulbs in the fall while dormant.

Dentaria laciniata.

BULBS FOR THE AUTUMN GARDEN

BY JUDY GLATTSTEIN

Most gardeners associate bulbs with the spring display provided by daffodils and tulips, crocus and snowdrops. Yet there are many other bulbs that flower at other times of year. It is especially rewarding to see new flowering in autumn, when most plants are going dormant. With autumn-flowering bulbs, planted in early autumn like spring-blooming bulbs, you need not wait months for flowers; a few weeks brings the gratification of bloom. Keep in mind, however, that because these bulbs will begin their growth right away, planting should be equally prompt; fall-blooming bulbs cannot sit around in brown paper bags until Thanksgiving, or even Halloween.

Some of these late-flowering species bloom "naked," unaccompanied by leaves. Thus it is a good idea to mark their location in some fashion, so that the spring flurry of clean-up and planting will not inadvertently disturb them. I have had great

JUDY GLATTSTEIN *is a freelance writer and an instructor at both BBG and New York Botanical Garden. She lives in Connecticut.*

success using a mat-forming groundcover of one kind or another as a "marker" — low-growing herbs such as *Thymus serpyllum* cultivars, for example. They have the added advantage of preventing autumn rains from splashing dirt onto the flowers and spoiling their appearance. And while in active growth in the summer, the groundcover will make use of moisture which the dormant bulbs do not need. What's more, I much prefer the look of plants in combination — especially in the instance of the autumn-blooming bulbs, most of which flower without leaves.

A major difficulty is obtaining the bulbs as early as August, as the books suggest. The earliest I have ever seen any of these in local nurseries, or received them by mail-order, is September. By this time many are showing pale, elongating shoots, fragile and susceptible to drying. Having chosen the planting location before I purchase the bulbs, I've cleared the first hurdle. Bulbs need more phosphorus and potassium than herbaceous plants, which do not have storage roots. I use muriate of potash and superphosphate, mixed into the bottom of

Colchicum.

the planting hole. Since these are both chemical salts and can harm the basal plate, it is important that the granules are well mixed with soil, and a thin layer of unfertilized soil should be added to reduce likelihood of contact. If you suspect the fertility of your soil is low, use a liquid fertilizer in subsequent years. Apply the fertilizer when the leaves are green and growing, to supply immediately available nutrients to the bulbs during their relatively short period of above-ground growth. My favorite is Peter's Blossom Booster (10-30-20). Apply it half-strength when the leaves first appear, and twice more at three-week intervals. This is probably more important in the lean gritty soils of a rock garden than in the humus-rich soils of woodland gardens.

Planting depth is generally three times the height of the bulb, deeper in sandy soil. Heavy clay soils require more shallow planting; however, such soils are generally too wet for healthy bulb growth and it would be better to select a different site. After planting, water thoroughly. Replace any disturbed mulch, and wait. Flowering should commence shortly.

Most popular of the autumn-flowering bulbs are the *Colchicum* species. The gobletlike flowers appear in September and October. Once pollinated they swoon and loll seductively on the ground. Fresh flowers appear for a couple of weeks, extending the flowering period. They are easily distinguished from crocus as colchicum have six stamens; crocus only three. The flower color is generally a soft mauve-lilac, sometimes checkered, depending on the species. White forms are sometimes available, and *Colchicum autumnale plenum* and *C. speciosum* 'Waterlily' are double-flowered forms. Coarse, broad, bright green straplike foliage appears in the spring and persists until mid-June when it turns yellow and collapses all over its neighbors. Because of this untidy habit, colchicums are best grown with shrubs or comparably vigorous associates. While pollination occurs in the autumn, seed does not appear until late May; this habit gave rise to the old vernacular name of "son before the father." Some delightful selections include: *Colchicum autumnale*, daintier than the other species and thus suitable for

Colchicum speciosum 'Album'.

Colchicum autumnale poking above *Athyrium goeringianum* 'Pictum'.

combination with ferns or some of the smaller hosta at the edge of a woodland; *C. bornmuelleri* with large flowers of good substance, the color deepening as the flowers mature; and *C. speciosum*, which has large raspberry-pink flowers with a white throat. *C. agrippinum* is the best available tessellated variety, with attractive, strongly checkered petals that make up for the rather weak perianth tube, which causes

Crocus speciosus.

Colchicum autumnale pleniflorum.

the flowers to fall over. Colchicums are the source of the drug colchicine, and are generally not eaten by pests.

It is with fall crocus that the garden truly receives a rejuvenation. With careful selection, crocus can be in bloom not only in spring and fall, but even in winter.

Non-gardeners, especially those with culinary interests, may be aware of the saffron crocus, *Crocus sativus*. It is the red

29

Crocus longiflorus.

stigmas of this crocus which are the source of the costly spice. While you can harvest enough to season an occasional paella, I hesitate to suggest that your fortune is made, as it takes approximately 4,000 flowers to produce one ounce. This is one crocus which does not seem to like my garden. Plump corms do well the first season, then dwindle and decline rapidly. With its rich purple flowers it is an attractive addition to the rock garden, if only it would persist.

Far more successful is *C. speciosus*. This has been in cultivation long enough that several selections are available — 'Aitchisonii', 'Cassiope' and 'Oxonian' are but a few. One of the earliest of the fall crocus, its lavender-blue flowers with a yellow throat appear in September. It is a prolific species, increasing by both seed and offset. The thin grasslike leaves are not a problem, even where it grows in profusion. They appear in spring, grow and fade away without harming nearby plants as colchicum might. I especially enjoy this bulb when grown with *Sedum sieboldii*, whose mauve-pink flowers overlap in blooming sequence with the crocus. At the edge of woodland I like *C. speciosus* mingled with

Ophiopogon planiscapus 'Nigrescens', whose deep black leaves are an elegant foil for the lavender chalices of the crocus.

One crocus which does flower accompanied by foliage is *C. longiflorus*. The yellow-throated purple flower has good substance, and a faint fragrance of violets. Faint, that is, if you expect a four-inch-tall flower to waft its perfume to your nose. Crawl around on your hands and knees and the scent will be much stronger. It is fortunate that this species is also a free increaser as, like all other crocus, it is a favorite with the deer. I console myself with the thought that in Greece it is the goats who dine on these plants I treasure. Small comfort, and it would be best to find a place where the crocus is protected. It is charming in combination with the foliage of dwarf geraniums such as *Geranium sanguineum* var. *prostratum*, or small ornamental grasses.

A white-flowered fall-blooming crocus is *C. ochroleucus*. This flowered for me in late October/early November. The flowers seemed too frail, too thin in texture for the season, although it was attractive as it blossomed through the hoary mat of *Thymus lanuginosus*. With good drainage during

Cyclamen.

the period of summer dormancy, it has been reasonably persistent. *C. niveus* is another white-flowered species with more rounded, gobletlike flowers.

Another autumn-flowering bulb is *Allium thunbergii*, a dainty onion from Japan with umbels of lilac flowers above grasslike foliage in October. This has no objectionable onion odor, and is more than welcome for its late bloom. It looks good with *Sedum sieboldii*, thymes, dianthus and other small-scale plants.

Colchicum, crocus and allium are plants for sunny or only lightly shaded sites. *Cyclamen hederifolium* (which used to be known as *C. neapolitanum*) is a plant for the deciduous woodland. The flowers appear first, in late August and early September, dancing on naked stems like badminton shuttlecocks or a flock of dainty pink butterflies. The leaves appear later in September, beautifully marked with silver. It seems that, like snowflakes, each tuber has a different pattern to its markings. The leaves remain through the winter and only fade into summer dormancy in late May/early June. This cyclamen has attractive foliage for nearly ten months of the year, certainly a good return for the space it occupies. This is one bulb worth cultivating for its foliage as well as its exquisite flower. Cyclamen require a soil rich in humus, moist but well-drained, in dappled shade. Plant them shallowly, only an inch or two deep, and mulch with leaf litter. The tuber neither splits, nor makes offsets, but rather grows larger in diameter and produces more flowers year by year. Generally seed is freely produced. I suggest you gather it, and sow it in a protected area, for mice, voles and chipmunks find the first-year tubers like toothsome pink caviar. This is an easy means of propagation and a sure source of plants which have not been collected in the wild. When the cyclamen is dormant in summer you could use the space for annuals such as impatiens, but be sure to remove the filler plants as soon as the cyclamen begin to grow.

When you are ordering bulbs, most assuredly look ahead to spring. But reward yourself with the more immediate pleasure of autumn-blooming bulbs.

THE INFORMATION IN THIS ARTICLE FIRST APPEARED IN DIFFERENT FORM IN *THE BULLETIN OF THE AMERICAN ROCK GARDEN SOCIETY*.

BULBS IN A
BUFFALO GRASS LAWN

BY SANDY SNYDER

Blue and purple irises and white crocus in dormant buffalo grass.

Bulbs in my xeriscape lawn have been a source of spring delight. Every year between the end of January and the end of April crocus, *Iris reticulata*, daffodils and tulips become a tapestry of color on the light brown, dormant buffalo grass lawn "canvas."

Because water conservation is important in Colorado, I converted my Kentucky bluegrass lawn to buffalo grass (*Buchloe dactyloides*). This grass is a warm-season, drought-tolerant grass that is easy to grow in hot, dry areas of the country. It requires much less water and fertilizer than a bluegrass lawn. The only disadvantage of this grass is that it takes about two months longer than Kentucky bluegrass to green up in spring. To solve this problem I added color by planting bulbs in the grass. Buffalo grass lends itself well to naturalizing bulbs because it grows only between four and six inches tall.

I chose bulbs native to areas in central Asia where the climate is similar to Denver's. In the fall of 1984 I planted about 2,500 crocus, iris, tulips and other bulbs.

The bulbs make a superb show of bloom in early spring. Then their leaves develop, making the lawn look green instead of brown. The bulb leaves turn yellow and die back about the time the buffalo grass starts growing, so I can have a regular lawn in the summer and early fall. Best of all, the bulbs multiply and make larger clumps each year. They have increased 20 to 30 fold in five years, and the cumulative impact is spectacular.

Our buffalo grass/bulb garden was an

SANDY SNYDER *gardens on three-quarters of an acre in Littleton, Colorado, as well as in the Rock Alpine Garden at Denver Botanic Gardens.*

Red *Tulipa linifolia* and pink *Tulipa humilis.*

experiment. We didn't know anyone who had done it before and could tell us what to expect. The combinations turned out so well that I'd like to encourage gardeners in thirsty climates throughout the Southwest to try similar plantings.

Aside from weeding, the buffalo grass has required much less maintenance than bluegrass. I usually mow the lawn for the first time sometime before July 4th. By that time all the bulb leaves are very dry or gone. After that I mow about once a month with the mower set to cut as high as possible — three inches. In the fall when the grass is dormant I mow it down to one and one half inches tall, so the flowers will show up better in the spring.

I considered several factors in choosing which bulbs to plant. I wanted species that would bloom early in the spring and die back by the end of June so mowing could begin. They had to be hardy in USDA Zone 5 (to -20⁰) and to naturalize well.

If you do not intend to mow the grass, but rather wish to keep it as an informal meadow, bulbs with larger flowers, leaves and stalks can be used. Crown imperials (*Fritillaria imperialis*) and foxtail lily or desert candle (*Eremurus*) are candidates for a large grassy meadow. *Calochortus* and *Brodiaea*, bulbs that bloom later in the spring and into the summer, can be used in a summer meadow that isn't mowed.

When the bulbs arrived I realized that I hadn't thought out how we were going to plant them without tearing up the lawn and devoting several days to the job. My husband Bill invented a planting tool — a broomstick with a two-by-four crosspiece step that can be adjusted to make holes of different depths. This pogo stick-like tool worked so well that we set up a three-person production line and planted all the bulbs in just a few hours. One person punched a hole in the sod. The second person dropped a bulb into the hole — some of the bulbs tipped upside down, but they all came up anyway. The third person filled the hole with dry sand (rather than lumpy soil), and we watered the whole area when we finished planting. We didn't add any bone meal to the soil because our bulbs arrived in October and we had to plant them in a hurry. It would have been too time consuming to mix the bone meal with soil, pour it in the little hole, pour a bit more soil in the small hole and then drop in the bulb. I think foliar feeding in the spring would be a good way to nourish the bulbs if you felt the soil was not rich enough.

We tried to plant the bulbs in natural patterns. The usual recommendation is to throw the bulbs up in the air and plant them where they fall. If we'd tried that method, we would have lost most of the fingertip-size bulbs in the grass. Instead, we designed two planting patterns. In one area we made spiral patterns, with the bulbs planted three to four inches apart in the center, gradually increasing the spacing to as much as 18 to 24 inches. The spirals were generally about ten feet across, and overlapped one another. We put one spiral in the center of the area, and six more at equal spacings in a circular pattern around the center one. Our other pattern was a series of six drifts, each planted with a different variety, that overlapped to make a long crescent shape. Here we also spaced the bulbs close together in the center of each drift and farther apart at the edges. Overlapping the different varieties in both planting patterns creates a more naturalistic effect. In retrospect, I'd say the spirals are more effective, and I'd suggest spacing them randomly around a lawn rather than grouping them as we did.

The snowdrops are always the first to bloom, and generally bloom for the longest time. They aren't as showy as the other species, but their earliness more than compensates. The different varieties of crocus bloom between mid- February and mid-April. The best effect usually comes around the end of March when the white and light-blue crocuses are still in bloom and the dark-blue and dark-purple irises open. Finally, in mid- to late-April the tulips open, and they normally last around two weeks. During spring snow often covers our lawn, but the flowers are not injured. In fact, it's delightful to see the colorful blooms against the white blanket of snow, each flower individually outlined. The irises show particularly well this way.

Mixing and matching different colors of blooms and combining bulbs that bloom at different times allow you to create artistic patterns and effects, but first you'll have to do some homework. Experiment with different species and varieties to find out how they do in your area; nearby private and public gardens are good sources of ideas. When we planned our planting patterns, we tried to put all the early-blooming bulbs in one group and the later bloomers in another area. Unfortunately, our actual bloom times varied greatly from those listed in the catalog so we had early and late bloomers in both areas. For that matter, the same bulbs I planted in my lawn I also planted in my steep, southwest-facing, stone-mulched rock garden, a much warmer microclimate in which they bloom at least a month earlier. One last note on blooming times: The first year's timing will most likely be quite different from that maintained in subsequent years.

All the bulbs have multiplied. The crocuses apparently increase by division. The first year each bulb made one flower; five years later there were 35 flowers in many crocus clumps. *Tulipa tarda* and *T. urumiensis* are the most vigorous multipliers. They produce lots of seeds, and the way their clumps are increasing indicates that the bulbs are dividing. Tulip seedlings hide in the grass, forming just one little leaf the first season. I haven't been able to track any, but I think they can flower after two or three years. Snowdrops make large green seedpods, but they don't increase very fast in my lawn; perhaps they prefer cooler, damper conditions. The dwarf daffodils, *Narcissus asturiensis*, are increasing slowly.

In a traditional garden the bulbs are dug up and divided every few years. Last year I marked several large clumps of crocuses and *Iris reticulata* with color-coded nails. I planned to dig them up after the leaves had died and spread the bulbs to some of my other gardens. I couldn't find the nails again, and I didn't want to dig holes all over the lawn trying to track down clusters of bulbs. So, for now, I have given up on the idea. I'll just let them spread as they may until they stop blooming because of overcrowding.

In June of 1990 I created an additional 800 square feet of buffalo grass lawn, and I'm compiling another bulb wish list. *Crocus tomasinianus* is a crocus I don't have in my spring flowering group, and I also want to add the 'Ruby Giant' crocus to my collection. The rest of my additions will be fall-blooming crocus because I don't want a summer meadow in this part of the yard: *Crocus medius*, with violet-purple blooms, *Crocus pulchellus*, with pink-lavender flowers, and *Crocus speciosus*, which comes in different shades of blue. In our spring collection we have observed that the bulbs that send up flowers before leaves show much better than the bulbs that send up the leaves and flowers together. Fall crocus send up their leaves in the spring. Only the brilliant flowers will dot the dormant grass in the fall.

Buffalo grass makes a very acceptable suburban lawn, and the bulbs make the lawn a seasonal delight. What's more, I feel that I am doing my part for water conservation, and saving money and work by converting my traditional bluegrass lawn to a new type of xeriscape landscaping. ✳

ADAPTED FROM AN ARTICLE THAT FIRST APPEARED IN *FINE GARDENING* MAGAZINE.

Tulipa tarda.

Tulipa humilis.

BULBS IN MASS PLANTINGS

BY HENRY J. EULER III

One of the great joys of spring is visiting public gardens to revel in the beauty of large, massed bulb displays. I make the pilgrimage to various gardens to affirm my belief that spring is truly a time of spiritual and physical awakening. The same effect can be created in your own garden. My small suburban lot (one-eighth of an acre) contains 1,500 bulbs including daffodils, chionodoxa, crocus, tulips and gladiolus. Another backyard garden of 280 square feet includes 250 daffodils mingled with woody and herbaceous plants. These small gardens provide a knockout punch of color each spring.

Before opening a bulb catalog, take a good hard look at your garden and inventory the unplanted spaces. For example, look at the foundation planting, and note any voids between plants that could be

HENRY J. EULER III *is Director of the School of Horticulture at the New York Botanical Garden. He also designs gardens from an office in Oyster Bay, New York.*

filled with bulbs. Select those that will complement the existing plants in color, size and scale. Avoid planting a single row of bulbs along the front edge of the bed.

Look over the plantings near the patio, deck or porch. These areas can be improved by tucking in a few minor bulbs followed by tulips, daffodils or fritillaria. After the spring bulbs, plant masses of caladiums, tuberous begonias, border dahlias, gloxinias or achimenes. The key to planting around patios, decks and other outdoor "rooms" is to use plants that flower or show color when the area is to be used. If the area will be used in the evening, be sure to include white, silver or variegated plants to add contrast to the nightscape.

A herbaceous border offers wonderful locations for massing bulbs. The most effective planting technique is to accent specimen plants with groups of bulbs. Daffodils, tulips or hyacinths are usually planted in groups of twelve, large bulbs like *Fritillaria imperalis, Lilium* or galtonias in groups of six and the minor bulbs in groups of three to four dozen. Allow ample room for the colonizers like crocus, chionodoxas, narcissus and montbretias. After flowering, bulb foliage will yellow and die. If this disturbs you, locate the bulbs so that the foliage of emerging perennials or woody plants will hide the dying leaves. Before deciding to naturalize bulbs in the lawn, remember that the bulb foliage must not be cut until it has matured or yellowed. In the New York metropolitan area this is around the first of July. By that time the grass could reach substantial height.

Be sure to note sites in the garden that will accommodate a naturalized planting. In naturalized areas try to capture the feeling that the plants grew and colonized without a helping hand. Excellent areas for naturalized plantings include the banks of brooks, edges of ponds, along paths and in orchards and meadows, under trees, beneath shrubs or the base of hedges, with ferns, along a wall and around the base of garden ornaments. To achieve the natural look, plant in irregular groups and use the same varieties in any one group. Excellent naturalizers include *Crocus, Colchicum, Scilla, Muscari, Lilium, Allium, Chionodoxa, Narcissus, Galanthus* and *Hyacinthus*.

With planting locations identified, the next consideration is plant combinations. Blue-flowered plants like *Scilla, Muscari* and *Chionodoxa* go well with shrubs like *Magnolia tomentosa (M. stellata), Hamamelis* species, *Forsythia* and *Prunus glandulosa*. A shrub border or wall shows tulips to best advantage. But their wide range of colors also complements *Wisteria, Syringa, Spiraea, Iberis, Berberis* and *Ilex*.

Narcissus offer a large and varied group of colors, heights and flower shapes, making them useful in most areas of the garden. They fit especially well around shrubs and with a little planning it is possible to have bloom over much of the spring sea-

son. The small cupped daffodils such as 'Actaea', 'Foundling' 'Cragford' 'April Tears' or 'Geranium' look wonderful under flowering trees and the miniatures like 'February Silver' 'Jack Snipe' and 'Tete-a-Tete' do well as accent plants for rock gardens and as edging plants. Use them in perennial borders or with ground covers such as ivy, *Ajuga, Vinca* or *Cotoneaster*. To add drama and delight to the garden, include some of the double-flowered daffodils ('Cheerfulness', 'White Lion' or 'Sir Winston Churchill') and fragrant daffodils ('Thalia', 'Cheerfulness', 'Baby Moon', 'Andalusia' or 'Pipit') in the bulb border.

Hyacinths have great appeal with their bold colors and fragrance. This versatile plant is often massed formally but lends itself to naturalizing in the border. Hyacinths combine well with *Arabis, Alyssum, Myosotis*, tulips and pansies.

The crocus offer a host of planting options. They grow well with low ground covers (*Vinca, Sedum, Ajuga, Euonymus* and *Hedera*, for example) that can support their flowers and protect them from being splattered with mud during rains. When planting crocus with ground covers, be sure the crocus will not be crowded over time. These little garden gems mass well under trees or shrubs and combine with *Eranthis* and *Chionodoxa*.

Select the bulbs that will fulfill the needs identified on the garden survey, including height, bloom period, color, foliage type and flower style and shape. Numerous bulb catalogs are available to assist the decision-making process.

After the bulbs are ordered and arrive, it is time for planting. Most bulb books discuss planting with either a trowel or a dibble. These tools work very well in situations where the soil has been prepared by rototiller or the bed has been in cultivation

PHOTOS BY HENRY EULER III

A golden mass of naturalized daffodils.

for a while. For planting in undisturbed soil, as in naturalizing bulbs, leave the trowel and dibble on the tool bench; a soil auger attached to an electric or gasoline-powered drill is a better tool for compacted soil. The only caution, learned from experience, is to watch out for sudden kick back from the drill if it runs into hard soil, rocks or roots. One tool to avoid is the common bulb planter, which looks like a can with both ends removed, on a shaft or handle. The low-cost versions break and the expensive models work as poorly as the less expensive ones. The problem is a basic design flaw that does not take the soil texture into account. Soils that have a high clay content tend to be difficult to dislodge from the cookie cutter-like planter, while sandy soils will inevitably fall through the device and be of no value for refilling the planting hole.

Daffodils lining pathways at a large estate.

Most gardeners have probably tried this device and if only a few bulbs were planted the job was finished before frustration caused the tool to be left curbside for garbage pick-up.

The most efficient, economical device for planting large numbers of bulbs is the common pick mattock. Do not confuse this tool with the cutter mattock. The pick mattock has two pointed ends, one shaped like a duck bill. The technique is simple and a two person team can plant bulbs at a rate of one every three to five seconds in light-textured soils. The person swinging the pick should kneel on the ground with the torso erect. The pick is swung in the same manner as in the standing position. The key to success is that the pick must enter the soil at a right angle. To reduce fatigue allow the weight of the pick to do the work. In soft ground the point of the pick will pierce the soil to a depth of seven to ten inches and in hard ground five to eight inches. With the point still in the ground, rock the pick back and forth to enlarge the hole, pulling forward to firm the soil and remove it from the hole. As the pick clears the hole the person planting the bulbs slips a bulb into the hole, making sure that the bulb makes contact with the bottom of the planting hole; then the operation is complete. It will take five or ten minutes to work out favorable positions for the picker and the planter. The most important point is that the person swinging the pick MUST ALWAYS have the planter in sight to avoid injury. As the team gains confidence the job will proceed at a rapid rate. To avoid fatigue switch positions after planting 100 or so bulbs.

Large bulbs, like lilies, can be planted quickly with a post hole digger. Lilies will require deeper planting than the smaller bulbs; the general rule is eight to ten inches deep. Plant deeper in sandy soils and less deep in heavy soils. Avoid sodden or wet areas totally as the bulbs will rot. The medium-sized bulbs — daffodils, tulips, hyacinths and fritillaria — prefer planting depths of four to seven inches, depending on the soil type per above. As a general rule, plant bulbs at a depth three times their height. For example, a one-inch bulb would require a planting hole three to four inches deep.

In natural settings space large bulbs nine to 12 inches apart, medium bulbs four to six inches apart and small bulbs three to five inches apart. Naturalized plantings are seldom divided or transplanted; allow ample room to grow.

Tulips are good candidates for formal planting but a poor choice for naturalizing. Some varieties may flower for five years, but most naturalized tulips will decrease in size and flower poorly after two to three years. To achieve maximum results with tulips, the bed should be excavated to a depth of six to eight inches. Loosen and rake smooth the soil in the bottom of the planting hole, add superphosphate at a rate of three pounds per 100 square feet, set the bulbs into the hole six inches on center and fill the area with soil, being careful not to knock over the bulbs. Planting tulips properly is labor intensive but the results are worth the trouble. The plants will be uniform in size. On large areas where it is totally impractical to remove the soil from the planting hole, prepare the soil by rototilling to a depth of eight inches and the bulbs can be planted with a trowel directly in the bed. One last consideration is weed control. The most satisfactory method is mulching.

On the north shore of Long Island experience has shown that the best time to fertilize bulbs is in the fall around the first week of November with a second feeding in the spring after flowering. It is a good idea to incorporate a phosphate-type fertilizer at the time of planting. This can be easily accomplished if the bulbs are to be planted in beds. For the naturalized planting, fertilize in the spring and the fall with either a chemical or organic fertilizer. Regardless of the product, read and follow the label directions. Take care when applying a fast-acting chemical fertilizer in a mixed planting of bulbs, shrubs and perennials. Avoid extended contact of the fertilizer and the foliage. For best results, wash the fertilizer into the soil with a hose or irrigation system.

If you follow these simple guidelines, spring and summer will be delightful and rewarding. A walk through your garden will be as pleasurable and satisfying as any public garden tour.

Bulb Guide According to Height

4" **TO** **8"**	*Galanthus* (Snowdrops)	white	EARLY SPRING
	Crocus	white blue purple yellow, striped	EARLY SPRING
	Anemone blanda	blue pink red white	APRIL-MAY
	Muscari	blue white	APRIL-MAY
	Species tulips	various colors	EARLY SPRING
8" **TO** **12"**	*Greigii* tulips	various colors	APRIL-MAY
	Kaufmanniana hybrid tulips	various colors	EARLY SPRING
	Hyacinths	various colors	APRIL
	Double early tulips	mixed colors	MID-APRIL
12" **TO** **20"**	Daffodils	mixed colors	APRIL-MAY
	Fosteriana tulips	various colors	EARLY SPRING
20" **TO** **30"**	Triumph tulips	mixed colors	APRIL-MAY
	Parrot tulips		
	Lily flowering tulips		
	Darwin hybrid tulips		
	Cottage tulips		
30" **+**	*Allium*	purple rose lilac white	APRIL-JULY
	Fritillaria	red yellow plum	APRIL-MAY

Fritillaria persica.

BULBS IN THE INFORMAL GARDEN

BY MADELEINE KEEVE

AND

JOHN EMMANUEL

The first recorded use of bulbs in an informal setting is found in The Iliad, Book 14. On a barren mountain in Turkey the goddess Hera, in an effort to assist the besieged people of Troy, seduces her consort, Zeus, who favors the opposing Greeks. The two immortals lie, Homer tells us, in a bed of hyacinths and crocus. No doubt the formal use of bulbs began with the mortals, who dug up these fleeting wildflowers, which they found in the mountains and cultivated in pots on their window ledges.

Whether you are scattering bulbs in a meadow or accommodating them in a tiny backyard, there is an infinite variety of plant combinations with which to create your own Olympic idyll. However, you must be patient and await the sometimes slow fruition of your efforts to create an informal garden. For 20 years the spectacle at the Wild Garden at Wave Hill has been unfolding, thanks to the cumulative planning of its gardeners. The mature trees and shrubs planted fifteen years ago (indeed, some of the trees go much further back) provide the necessary structure for the seasonal drama of the herbaceous plantings.

Fritillaria imperialis.

MADELEINE KEEVE AND JOHN EMMANUEL *are gardeners at Wave Hill in New York City.*

Canna.

The Wild Garden is divided by a series of narrow winding paths into fourteen variously shaped beds covering a hillside. Foils for the herbaceous plants, the trees, shrubs and large stands of grasses divide the beds into many diverse tableaux. As visitors round each corner, a new tableau appears. While tiny *Tulipa batalinii* grows in a south-facing dry bed, *Fritillaria imperialis* (crown imperial fritillary) towers not far off in a lush enclave in the shade of an *Amelanchier canadensis* (shadbush), which divides one bed from another. Months later in another bed, the giant leaves of the tropical tuber, *Colocasia esculenta* (elephant's ear) extend beyond a large rock where they contrast with a wonderful variegated *Yucca* 'Bright Edge' that grows amid a sprawling *Cedrus deodara* 'Prostrata' (prostrate deodar cedar).

In a formal garden, where spring tulips are massed in unified colors, the gardener hopes for a spectacle that will remain relatively fixed in time. In the informal garden, on the other hand, change is the force which the gardener must use to great advantage. Often as a plant unfolds it reveals aspects of its personality which work perfectly, for a moment, with the characteristics of a neighboring plant. For example, in one of our beds *Penstemon venustus azureus* begins the season as a rosette of vibrant purple red leaves, perfectly suited to the small purple *Iris pumila*. Later the penstemon, now bearing its developing flower stalks of dark red, encounters the diminutive *Narcissius* with its flat, pale yellow flowers. By mid-May, with its spires bearing pendulous lavender flower buds, the penstemon blends well with the late-blooming, brilliant red *Tulipa sprengeri*. When at last the penstemon's lavender flowers are fully open in early June, it's worthy of admiration on its own merits. Every plant offers a thousand faces against which any number of other plants, also changing, can work for a moment. The principle underlying the creation of these scenes is the understanding that bulbs co-exist happily with a wide range of plants.

In another grouping *Narcissus* 'Sun Disc' draws *Aurinia saxatilis* (basket of gold) out of its shabby winter attire to its peak of spring beauty. And it needn't be *N.* 'Sun Disc'; any diminutive narcissus of your liking might do. We happen to have *N.* 'April Tears' growing nearby *Iris pallida* 'Variegata'. The two seem to strike it off with a medley of yellows and greens. But what if the *Iris* were *Acorus calamus* 'Variegata' or the pale leaves of a sprouting *Liriope spicata* 'Silver Dragon'? For the gardener willing to chance a bad combination, the opportunities of discovering a good one are endless.

One of the persistent challenges of using bulbs informally is attending to the ripening foliage which must not be cut to ensure the bulbs' survival. The scale of a planting will often determine what looks

Chionodoxa luciliae.

good. For example, where daffodils are naturalized in a meadow on a large scale, yellowing foliage in the uncut grass does not seem unruly. At close hand in a small garden, though, it can be a problem. Because we combine bulbs with a variety of other plants, we try to find ways to hide the dying leaves. Sometimes their ungainly foliage (daffodils being a prime example) can be tucked beneath neighboring plants. More often than not, the foliage is tolerable because there is so much going on in the vicinity. Occasionally you can even use the ripening seed heads to advantage. For example, *Allium karataviense* rises out of two broad, striped basal leaves of a bluish hue. As the allium dries, both the leaves and the flower heads pass through various stages of pink, which combine well with the glaucous foliage of nearby *Crambe maritima, Glaucium flavum* and other silver-foliage plants.

After the rush of spring, summer and fall bulbs offer an often unexplored realm of possibilities. Lilies are among the first to bloom in the Wild Garden. Between the blue-needled limbs of *Pinus flexilis* 'Glauca Pendula' (prostrate blue limber pine), *Lilium* x *dalhansonii*, a copper-colored lily spotted with purple, appears, towering over the low-lying limbs. *Clematis* 'Betty Corning' scrambles over the pine, casting its pendant purple bells like a net under the lily. Because 'Betty Corning' blooms for a long time, *L.* x *dalhansonii* is only one of several lilies we use to create a continuum of bloom. You *can* plant closely, if you keep an eye on things and make sure that plants don't smother one another.

Sylvia Crowe once wrote: "Garden features are far more often too small than too big." Two examples in the Wild Garden that illustrate this idea feature tropical plants that never bloom for us. In both cases they are large plants growing in small spaces for dramatic effect. The aforementioned *Colocasia esculenta* growing between the yucca and *Juniperus rigida* is one example. Another is *Dahlia imperialis*, which grows to an impressive 15 feet before the first frost kills the foliage. In front of the treelike dahlia, we mass cannas with strong linear red leaves. Vining *Gloriosa rothschildiana* (gloriosa lily) tumbles over old iris leaves nearby.

One of the biggest problems gardeners face with bulbs is planning ahead. The moment of inspiration often comes when the plants are blooming, while the moment to plant bulbs comes months later. When we made a note back in early spring to add *Fritillaria imperialis* 'Aurea' to Bed A, the bed was a clear slate bearing the existing *Fritillaria*, a group of yellow narcissus and clusters of *Chionodoxa luciliae*. But by August the bed was overgrown with the spires of countless perennials. To avoid this kind of confusion, we often plant unfamiliar bulbs in a test bed. When they come into bloom we get ideas. That is when we move them in among suitable companions in the Wild Garden. The desired effect is immediate. Where a garden picture no longer works, or where bulbs are overgrown by shrubbery, we feel free to move bulbs after they make their appearance. Spring planting also avoids the danger of cutting into bulbs already present — a frequent occurrence when bulbs are added to others in the fall. In the case of the *Fritillaria*, which we already know and want to increase, we fix green stakes in the desired locations in spring, when the ground is still a clean slate. When the bulbs arrive in the fall, we know exactly where to plant them, despite the abundance of autumn camouflage.

In the case of *Canna, Colocasia, Dahlia* and other summer bulbs, which must all be dug up and stored in a cool location after the first frost, spring planting is a *sine qua non*, and their placement requires a familiarity with their habits. If they are new to you, don't be afraid to experiment with them; you can always plant them in a new spot next year. One year, a colocasia was accidentally planted among some cannas at the edge of a path. The result was spectacular, proving that accidents can lead to wonderful discoveries.

An informal garden should not be mistaken for a low-maintenance garden. Since change is the great operating force, the gardener must keep a constant watch, day to day, lest the wonderful tapestry of plants come undone by one or two weedy species. For example, *Endymion hispanicus* is a proven thug (albeit a lovely one), so it has been banished to the rough outskirts of the garden, where it can spread happily beneath trees. Be vigilant, but not intimidated. While change brings on the weeds and rush of growth that stagger us at the beginning of every season, it also brings new visions and new inspiration.

Lycoris squamigera.

DAFFODILS

BY JUDY GLATTSTEIN

Daffodils are perhaps the most widely recognized of bulbs. They are common in gardens and among the first flowers we learn to recognize as children. Spring always seems to have arrived when I see bunches of golden daffodils and branches of pussy willow for sale. In autumn, the big, brown onionlike daffodil bulbs provide a promise of flowers after winter's end. Readily obtainable, simple to plant, reliable in flower, what more could be asked? Some thought is required on how to make effective use of their bright spring display, and conceal the yellowing foliage later on.

"Daffodil" is merely a common name for *Narcissus*. This confusion is sometimes compounded by the use of "jonquil," especially in the South, to refer to the common daffodil, when there is a separate division among daffodils, the jonquilla narcissi. All the different groupings of daffodils depend on the form of the flower: relative length of cup to petals, shape of the cup, etc.

Use daffodils in groups of ten or more of a kind. Plant three times as deep as the bulb is high, perhaps a little deeper in light sandy soil, more shallowly in heavy clay. While daffodils can tolerate very moist soils while in growth, winter wet can lead to bulb rot. Avoid planting in heavy wet soils; either plant in a different location or make a raised bed to improve drainage. Rather than use the so-called naturalizing mixtures which flower in random display, I prefer to buy separate varieties and plant them in distinct groups. This allows me to create some pattern, more effective than a spotty effect. Daffodils planted in a woodland have a tendency to face the sun while in bloom. This means if they are planted on both sides of a path running east-west, those on the north side of the path will face it while those on the south side will face away from the path. This is less noticeable in open situations.

Daffodils can be used in many different ways. They are elegant in a formal border, mingled with peonies and daylilies to disguise the aging bulb foliage. It is a poor technique to fold, braid or tie up bulb foliage as it reduces the ability of the leaves to send food down to the bulb for the next year's bloom. As was indicated, daffodils are very suitable as woodland plants, used with hosta and ferns for companion plants to hide their old yellowing leaves. Daffodils can be planted in grass, but then the grass should not be mown until the bulb foliage has ripened. Thus a coarse grass situation such as in an orchard or a meadow is more suitable than a lawn right next to the house.

It is the trumpet daffodil, with one flower per stem and a cup equal to or longer than the petals, which is most familiar. This is the "host of golden daffodils" of Wordsworth, the daffodil spilling down the grassy hill at the Brooklyn Botanic Garden, the cut flower of the florist. Many cultivars exist, in variations on the theme of yellow, white and bicolor. 'King Alfred', 'Dutch Master' and 'Unsurpassable' are sunshine yellow, 'Beersheba' and 'Mt. Hood' are classic white and there are bicolors such as 'Spellbinder' with white trumpet and lemon yellow petals. The pink trumpet daffodils have the best color when the flower first opens and under cool conditions, so they are best used in a shaded situation.

Long-cup daffodils also have one flower per stem, but the cup is less than equal to the petals. The flowers can be yellow as in 'Carlton', white as in 'Ice Follies', or bicolor as 'Carbineer' with an orange cup and yellow petals or 'Louise de Coligny' with white petals and apricot pink cup.

Short-cup daffodils have one flower per stem, with a cup a third less than the length of the petals. 'Birima' has an orange cup and yellow petals; 'Audubon' has a pale yellow cup edged with orange-red and white petals.

Next come the double daffodils, with no regard to the proportion of cup to petals. 'Earlicheer' is ivory white with some lemon yellow petals mixed in; 'White Lion' is waxy white with some pale yellow petals in the center; 'Golden Ducat' is a sport of 'King Alfred' and just as golden yellow.

Triandrus daffodils have *N. triandrus* as a parent, and like the species have several small, nodding white to pale yellow flowers per stem. 'Angel's Tears' is white.

Cyclamineus daffodils come from *N. cyclamineus* and have petals that reflex back, "like a mule about to kick," according to one old book. These hybrids prefer partial shade and a soil which does not dry out in summer. 'February Gold' is yellow, flowering in late March or early April in my Connecticut garden; 'Peeping Tom' is also yellow; 'Jenny' is white. These are lower growing cultivars, often a foot or less in height.

Jonquils, the *N. jonquilla* hybrids, grow 8 to 18 inches tall and have two to six sweetly fragrant flowers later in the season. 'Pipit' opens a soft lemon yellow with the cup fading to white; 'Quail' is soft golden yellow; 'Baby Moon' is buttercup yellow and 'Lintie' has an orange-yellow cup and yellow petals.

Paperwhite narcissus, familiar for coaxing into winter bloom indoors in a bowl of pebbles, helping restless gardeners survive the winter, are tazetta daffodils, bunch-flowering hybrids of *N. tazetta* with four to eight or more sweetly scented flowers to a stem. These are best used outdoors in the South and for indoor bloom in cold winter regions, as they are less hardy than the other groups. 'Bridal Crown' is a double white; 'Cragford' has an orange cup and cream-white petals; 'Geranium' has a geranium red cup and white petals; and the familiar 'Paperwhite" (a generic name) and 'Soleil d'Or', sometimes called Chinese sacred lily, are familiar white and bicolor yellow-and-white varieties. If grown indoors in pebbles and water, they should be discarded after flowering for they've exhausted food reserves and will be too weakened to salvage for another season.

Pheasant's eye daffodil, *N. poeticus*, flowers in May. The flowers, one per stem, have a small ruffle of a cup, pale yellow edged with red, and white petals. 'Actaea'

Daffodils and primroses line a rustic wood fence.

is an old variety which I've found surviving and flowering in long abandoned gardens under brambles. 'Cantabile' has a green cup rimmed deep red.

The split corona or butterfly daffodils have the cup torn into segments, often laid flat against the petals, giving the appearance of a daisy. 'Cassata' has a white "cup" tipped with pale yellow and white petals; 'Pico Bello' has a white "cup" tipped with central orange band and white petals; 'Valdrome' has a deeper yellow "cup" and soft yellow petals. The daffodils in this category seem less persistent than, say, trumpet or poeticus cultivars. I use them in more formal settings rather than woodland or naturalized groupings.

Species daffodils are any which occur wild. Here are grouped *N. cyclamineus, jonquilla, tazetta* and others, some of which are parents of the hybrids. There is, as might be expected, a good deal of diversity. The hoop petticoat daffodil, *N. bulbocodium,* grows eight inches tall with a funnel-shaped cup and petals reduced to narrow spikes. As it prefers full sun and a sandy gritty soil, this would be a good choice for the rock garden. *N. asturiensis*

(*N. minimus*) is a miniature of the trumpet daffodils, growing only three to four inches tall with a perfect little yellow trumpet. I've had this absolutely hardy flower outdoors in late February or early March. The dainty size makes it suited for use in pots, flowering year after year under alpine house or cold frame conditions. *N. pseudonarcissus* is the Lent lily, found wild in English woodlands in March. About 12 inches tall, the trumpetlike flowers have a lemon yellow cup and sulphur yellow petals.

Daffodils have much to recommend them. They are reliable in bloom, often making offsets and increasing in number from year to year. They can be grown in sunny situations provided the soil does not bake dry in summer, and are at home in deciduous woodlands. Most are hardy in cold winter areas, and there are varieties which tolerate mild winters. The flowers are excellent for cutting; bulbs can be coaxed into early bloom indoors. Better yet, daffodils are pest free, untouched by voles, chipmunks, mice, rabbits or deer. So excellent a plant should find its place in any garden, to brighten the spring scene year after year.

A massed meadow planting of daffodils.

EXPANDING YOUR INDOOR BULB COLLECTION

BY NAOMI BAROTZ

For plant lovers in the cold climes of the northern United States and Canada, growing bulbs indoors in containers can brighten the seemingly interminable dormant winter and spring months. There is something almost magical about watching a pot of paperwhite narcissus emerge into a delicate, fragrant bouquet, or in seeing the tropical *Hippeastrum* flower open on Christmas day. Among the wide variety of bulbous plants suitable for pot culture, the tender bulbs native to southern Africa offer the amateur grower a particularly rewarding challenge. Bulbs from this part of the world have been in cultivation for centuries. Many, like *Freesia* and *Gladiolus* hybrids, have made important contributions to the horticultural industry. However, the list of ornamental bulbs from southern Africa includes an incredibly rich and diverse selection of wildflowers

NAOMI BAROTZ *is Curator of the Desert Plant Collection at the New York Botanical Garden. In addition to cacti and other succulents, she enjoys growing tender bulbs from southern Africa and South America.*

highly valued for their spectacular beauty.

Some of these bulbs have been grown in the New York Botanical Garden greenhouses for over 30 years. Each year as winter sets in on the Garden grounds, pots of unusual bulbs from South Africa, Namibia, Swaziland and Botswana come into flower inside the Enid A. Haupt Conservatory, and the brilliant array of winter color lasts well into late spring.

Here is an overview of important guidelines for container cultivation, followed by a discussion of notable plants.

Cultural Guidelines

POTTING — Many of the southern African bulbs begin their growing season in our autumn. Bulbs stored in bags in cool, dry, well ventilated areas during their summer dormant period should be repotted during the fall months, preferably before any new shoots have begun to develop, as the new growth is very tender and easily broken. For most, clay pots are preferable to plastic both because of their porosity and their aesthetic qualities. The majority of these deciduous bulbs should be grown in a well

54

Hippeastrum.

drained, sandy potting soil that is slightly acidic. The basic mixture consists of about one-third sandy loam, one-third leaf mold and one-third sand, with bone meal added.

READING THE SIGNS — A proper watering schedule is critical, as many of these bulbs have distinct dormant and active growing periods. It is important to understand this cycle when growing bulbs in containers. After potting-up, the containers should be thoroughly watered only once. Regular watering should begin only when there are signs of growth. Excessive watering before growth has begun can cause bulb rot. Depending on the species, either new foliage or flower buds will appear first, or as in the case of some *Nerine* species and cultivars, both will appear at the same time. This new growth signals the end of the plant's dormant period. Watering can slowly begin, becoming more regular as the growth rate increases. Once the bulbs have begun to grow actively, they should be kept evenly moist but not soggy, and should not be allowed to dry out.

TEMPERATURE & LIGHT — Most of these bulbs are actively growing during the winter months and require full sunlight. The nighttime temperature should be between 40 and 45 degrees F and the daytime temperature between 50 and 55 degrees F. As the plants begin to go dormant during late spring and early summer, the greenhouse should be shaded; pots should not bake in the hot summer sun under glass. If shading is impossible, the pots should be moved to a shadier location or the bulbs should be lifted from their pots and stored.

The evergreen and summer-growing species also benefit from partially shaded growing conditions during the summer months. It is important to note that some species, especially those with fleshy roots, many of which are in the Amaryllis family, should not be lifted from their containers each summer; these fleshy-rooted species prefer to remain in their pots during the dormant cycle.

FERTILIZING — Many southern African bulbous species grow in nutrient poor soils in their native habitats. But when they are grown in containers, a proper fertilizing program is beneficial. Generally, fertilizing

55

Veltheimia.

should begin when the foliage is established and continue through flowering until the plants begin to show signs of entering dormancy. As a general rule, use a complete, low-nitrogen fertilizer bi-weekly at one-half strength. It is important to keep in mind that excess nitrogen will produce soft growth susceptible to disease. Since most of these plants are in active growth during the winter months in a cool environment where soil temperatures are often below 60 degrees F and watering is less frequent, urea and ammonium nitrogen used in many fertilizers can build up and injure the plant. Nitrate nitrogen liquid fertilizers or slow-release organic fertilizers are better choices. Some of the species, particularly those in the iris family, are sensitive to excess fluoride; burning of leaf margins or tips is the usual symptom. Have the fluoride level of your water tested. High levels

Clivia miniata.

Nerine hybrids.

can be reduced with a water filter. Avoid using materials such as perlite and super-phosphate. In addition, research has shown that fluoride-sensitive plants are more susceptible to fluoride toxicity when the soil pH is below 6.0.

DORMANCY — After the plants have flowered, the foliage will begin to yellow and die back, signaling the onset of dormancy. Some species do this more quickly than others. As the leaves yellow, decrease watering gradually until the bulbs have fully entered their resting stage, at which time watering should be stopped. At this time — late spring to early summer for most winter-growing species — the pots can be cleaned of dead foliage and flower stalks.

Freesia x *hybrida* 'Yellow'.

The Plants

THE IRIS FAMILY — *Freesia*, a small, but favored genus, is easy to grow in containers. Its arching spikes of sweetly scented flowers bloom from late winter through early spring. The flowers of the freesia hybrids are often larger and more colorful than many of the wild species. However, the species are usually more delicately marked and have sweeter scents. For example, the flowers of *Freesia alba* are white with a soft purple tinge and pale yellow markings. When potted in early September, this fragrant species flowers in mid-January. *F. refracta* has flowers with a wonderful spicy scent, which hang gracefully from a one-foot stalk. *Freesia* corms should be planted about two inches apart, one and one-half inches deep in a six-inch pot. Staggering the potting throughout the fall will extend the flowering period into late spring.

More than 100 species of gladiolus are native to southern Africa, of which about 70 species grow in the winter-rainfall areas of the Cape Province in South Africa. This group of gladiolus does quite well in the greenhouse and offers a wide variety of beautifully colored, graceful flowers. In late February, *Gladiolus orchidiflorus* displays its fragrant, elegant flowers. Its branched spikes of greenish-gray blooms are marked with a pastel purple. The icy-pink, frilly flowers of *G. carneus* or "painted lady" have deep scarlet blotches. *G. tristis* is a larger but striking container plant. Its soft-yellow flowers, which hang from 18 to 24 inch stalks, are wonderfully fragrant during the early evening hours.

Mid-March is the peak period for showy *Sparaxis tricolor*, harlequin flower. The orange-red, starlike flowers with their yellow centers marked with black are brilliant. *Sparaxis* hybrids, more often available

through the trade than the species, are equally stunning container plants.

The long wiry stalks of *Ixia*, the South African corn lily, support beautiful clusters of richly colored, starry flowers. Many *Ixia* species and striking new cultivars are well suited for container culture. Pot the corms of *Ixia dubia* in early fall, about one inch below the soil, with five to eight corms in a six-inch pot. Toward the end of April, brilliant yellow-orange flowers marked with dark centers come into bloom.

Another beautiful African genus is *Babiana* or baboon flower, so named because in its habitat, the edible corm is favored by baboons and other wild animals. Many *Babiana* species make excellent pot plants. The pleated, often hairy foliage is an added attraction to the rich-colored flower spikes. The royal blue flowers of *Babiana rubrocyanea* are accented with red centers. Planted about one inch deep, the corms should be potted up in early September; the first flower bud opens in mid-February. Another favorite species is *B. villosa,* which blooms in early spring. Its ruby-red to purplish flowers are accented by large dark anthers.

THE LILY FAMILY — For several centuries in Europe, *Lachenalia*, Cape cowslips, have been cultivated in pots as well as the garden. This large genus displays considerable variation in both foliage, flower and bloom period, which ranges from October to early May. The small, fleshy bulbs should be planted in shallow pots about one-half inch deep. The red-flowered *Lachenalia rubida* is one of the earliest flowering species. The larger, pendulous flowers of *L. bulbifera* are reddish-orange tipped with green and bloom in mid-winter. Later in spring, *L. contaminata* creates a splendid display with small white, bell-shaped flowers clustered against the dense growth of slender foliage.

There are only two species in the South African genus *Veltheimia*, both of which make wonderful pot plants. In early fall, the bulbs should be watered only when the dark-green to bluish-green leaves begin to appear. By mid to late winter, numerous pinkish tubular flowers hang from a fleshy, 18-inch stalk. Both *V. capensis* and *V. bracteata* require a dry dormant period in summer.

THE AMARYLLIS FAMILY — From late August through early November, pots of flowering South African nerines fill NYBG's greenhouse. The brilliant flower clusters in iridescent shades of pink, purple and red are a vivid reminder that the growing season for many of these tender bulbs has begun. Like many of the bulbs in the Amaryllis family, nerines do not prefer to be repotted each year. Instead, top-dress the pots with fresh soil just before dormancy ends. A dry, dormant period is important. Along with the more popular species such as *Nerine sarniensis* and *N. bowdenii*, a large selection of *Nerine* cultivars is available, offering a wide range of flower forms and color.

Haemanthus, another unusual southern African endemic, is an exotic addition to any collection. In early fall, the paintbrush lily, *Haemanthus coccineus*, produces a dense, scarlet-red flower cluster just before the two straplike leaves appear. The pair of thick, leathery leaves measure up to two feet long and eight inches wide and go dormant in early summer. *H. albiflos*, with white flowers and yellow anthers, is an evergreen species. Both species prefer a rich but well drained soil, with about one-third of the bulb exposed.

One of the more familiar and greatly admired greenhouse plants from southern Africa is *Clivia*. This evergreen plant prefers semi-shade and somewhat warmer winter temperatures than most of the other bulbous plants. Both *Clivia miniata* and *C. nobilis* are valued for their long-lasting flowers which bloom from late winter through spring. From the fans of long, strap-shaped leaves grow strong, fleshy stalks bearing dense umbels of magnificent orange tubular flowers.

CYCLAMEN FOR GARDEN USE

BY NANCY GOODWIN

One of the wonderful things about cyclamen is that you can have them blooming in the garden almost every day of the year. There are 19 known species, but I will write about the hardy ones that are easier to grow. Because more of them bloom in the fall than any other season, I consider that the beginning of the year. In the hot and humid Southeast the cool, clear air of fall provides the same excitement and renewed energy and enthusiasm for gardening that our northern friends experience with the first warm days of spring.

Cyclamen are easy to grow; in fact, they thrive on benign neglect. They insist on excellent drainage and some shade, but aren't fussy about soil pH. If you have heavy clay soil, add gravel and lots of humus to lighten it, or make a raised bed

NANCY GOODWIN *is proprietor of Montrose Nursery in North Carolina, a small mail-order nursery specializing in cyclamen and other unusual perennials — all propagated at the nursery. She has written articles for a number of journals and most recently has edited with Allen Lacy* A Rock Garden in the South *by Elizabeth Lawrence, published by the Duke University Press.*

with stones mixed in the soil. Be sure to plant the tubers away from an automatic watering system. Too much water is the surest way to kill them. Plant *Cyclamen repandum* about two to three inches deep, but most of the others are happiest right at soil level. They all go dormant for part of each year, so expect the same yellowing of foliage that is normal on narcissus, but causes alarm in new cyclamaniacs. I fertilize the plants in the garden with a general all-purpose fertilizer such as 8-8-8 when they begin to grow, and for most species that is in the fall.

Cyclamen are excellent grown in combination with other small bulbs. *C. coum* looks stunning with *Galanthus nivalis, Crocus sieberi* and *C. tomasinianus,* and in my garden some of the fall crocuses, such as *C. speciosus,* mingle handsomely with *C. hederifolium* and *C. graecum.* They are attractive with ferns and small hostas, but be sure to select the smaller cultivars and species that won't smother the more delicate cyclamen. *Helleborus orientalis, H. niger* and *H. foetidus* are all happy in the same situation, and they provide foliage when cyclamen are resting in the summer.

Cyclamen hederifolium is especially cheerful for it may bloom as early as May,

Cyclamen.

giving us one of the first signs of the fall season ahead. I have often wondered just what trigger mechanism stimulates the production of these elegant flowers with their swept-back petals. I believe it is a change in temperature. When days and nights become only a little cooler, after a period of warm weather, a few flowers of this species may be found. The year 1990, for instance, was strange in many ways,

61

with very warm weather in winter and a spring that alternated between hotter than normal and colder than normal temperatures. *C. hederifolium* was blooming by mid-May, and it didn't stop until November. The peak of bloom is from late August through October, and then the woodland floor is carpeted with masses of pink or white flowers, many of which are fragrant. The flowers precede the leaves, and in mid-fall the appearance of infinitely variable leaves signals an end to the production of flowers. Building a collection of different leaf forms is a temptation few can resist. They come in many shapes, from elongated sword forms, to ivy ones, nearly round and heartshaped. The colors and patterns of variegation go from dark green to silver, with many combinations in between.

C. graecum blooms at about the same time as *C. hederifolium*, often producing flowers in July and August but is at its peak of bloom in September. It has been a pleasant discovery that this species is hardy enough to grow in the cold part of Zone 7 where I am gardening. It has survived our record cold of -12 degrees F with no protection. This cyclamen is one of the few that is identifiable as a dried tuber. The tuber itself is corky and the roots are large and fleshy, unlike those of any other species. It grows in Greece in stony, sunny areas, and I am growing it in considerable sun on the south side of a large *Cedrus deodara*. The flowers are similar to those of *C. hederifolium*, but there are darker red-violet veins on the petals and the interior of the mouth is grape-colored. The leaves have a velvety sheen and are variable; some are all silver.

Just as the leaves are beginning to appear on *C. hederifolium* the flowers of *C. cilicium, mirabile* and *intaminatum* may be seen throughout the garden. These three species are closely related. In fact, *C. intaminatum* was considered a subspecies of *C. cilicium* until recently. Both *C. cilicium* and *mirabile* produce their leaves shortly before or with their flowers, but the third one has its flowers first. *C. intaminatum* is truly a miniature plant; the flowers are about one-half inch long and are white or very pale pink with tiny gray veins that don't make it look dingy. The leaves are round with beautiful patterns of silver or dark green. *C. cilicium* and *mirabile* have elegant flowers often with twisted petals in shades of red-violet to pure white, and their leaves are usually exquisitely marked in patterns of silver. *C. mirabile* has petals with fimbriated tips and somewhat angular leaves. These three species will provide flowers until well into December when *C. coum* takes over.

Winter-flowering cyclamen provide interest and color in the garden when there is little else. They make visits to the woods, even on cold days, worth bundling up for because the flowers can tolerate 10 degrees F. Because of the extraordinary number of distinct forms, we have planted areas of them in many different sections of the garden and they have been happy everywhere. We have them under a redbud, *Cercis canadensis*, on the north side of *Cedrus deodara*, in a stony rock garden just to the north of a large *Quercus alba*, and on a steep hillside in the woods beneath *Juniperus virginiana, Cornus florida* and *Carya ovata*. The flowers may be white, pink or dark magenta, all of which are attractive, but the dark ones show up best against the fallen, brown leaves or snow. Here, too, leaf patterns vary from silver with tiny green veins and a slender green margin to dark green with no variegation at all. The leaves precede the flowers by several months. It is tantalizing to see the buds weeks before the flowers finally open.

Cyclamen libanoticum has also proven hardy growing under *Cornus florida* in our woods. It has the distressing habit of losing its marbled, pewter-colored leaves if there is a prolonged cold spell, but its tubers remain firm. The flowers are large, and of an unusual shade of salmon-pink with attractive, darker bird-in-flight patterns at the base of each petal.

C. pseudibericum has the most impressive, showy flowers of any hardy cyclamen. It blooms from late winter through early spring. The flower color varies from pink through dark red-violet and the flowers have an almost black marking just above the white base of each petal. I am growing them with a mass of blue *Anemone blanda* under a pear tree that blooms at the same time, and the combination is splendid.

C. repandum with its twisted, medium-pink, fragrant flowers is the last of the spring-flowering, hardy cyclamen. Its ivy-shaped leaves often appear as early as February in North Carolina, but the flowers are present in March and April and plants go dormant shortly thereafter. This is one of the few species that needs to be planted about two to three inches below ground and that insists on shade.

Throughout the summer *C. purpurascens* blooms continuously, thus completing the year of flowering cyclamen. Although this is the hardiest of all the species, it isn't the easiest one to establish. It needs shade, and some moisture, but when established, is a constant joy, for unlike the others it requires only a week or so of dormancy. The new leaves appear just as the old ones are disappearing. All of the flowers are wonderfully fragrant, and the heart-shaped leaves look so much like wild ginger, *Asarum virginicum*, that the easiest way to distinguish them is by crushing a leaf and smelling it; asarum is the fragrant one. I am growing this cyclamen under a very large *Magnolia acuminata* and in the woods beneath *Quercus alba*.

The genus cyclamen is considered threatened throughout the world. The number of collected tubers exported from Turkey alone had risen from 256,000 in 1976 to over 6,600,000 in 1985. Although the European Community set an import quota of one million tubers from Turkey, we know that shortly thereafter, 1.6 million were imported by the Netherlands, and from March, 1988 to February, 1989 nearly 80,000 collected tubers were sent to the United States via Holland. It is a crisis, for dried-off tubers seldom grow, and although some species are in good supply, collectors can't distinguish between rare ones and the others. The importation of cyclamen now requires federal permits that state the origin of the tubers.

The solution is simple: Don't buy the large, dry tubers found in garden centers and mail-order nurseries throughout much of the world. Grow them from seed or purchase them from nurseries that propagate them. Seed sowing is easy; it just requires patience. The seeds should be soaked for about six hours, then sown covered by about one-quarter inch of potting soil. They germinate best in darkness, so cover the flats with plastic wrap and newspapers, or set them in a dark closet or basement. The seedlings will appear anytime from six weeks to about three years, generally at about the same time the species is coming back into growth after dormancy. The plants may be expected to bloom in two to three years, and once established in the garden will self sow and spread throughout the woodland, appearing in expected and often unexpected places.

Zantedeschia aethiopica in its natural habitat.

SOUTH AFRICAN BULBS FOR CALIFORNIA GARDENS

BY ROBERT ORNDUFF

South Africa supports the most spectacular, most diverse and richest bulb flora of any region of the world — with well over a thousand species of plants with bulbs or bulblike underground parts. Indeed, there are 200 native species of *Oxalis* alone, all with bulbs, and most with ornamental qualities. Most South African bulbous species occur in the winter-rainfall area of the Cape Province, such as members of *Lachenalia* and *Gladiolus*, which are concentrated there. However, there are substantial numbers of species in the summer-rainfall area that occupies most of South Africa, such as *Agapanthus* and *Kniphofia*. There is a narrow zone between these two areas, where rain is scant, but falls both in summer and winter. In the winter-rainfall area, most rain falls between April and September, equivalent to the period between October and March in the northern hemisphere, although the rainy season in our hemisphere is often longer by a month or two. Summers are long, dry and often hot. The winters are mild, though in some upland or interior regions of South Africa there are occasional severe frosts and even snow. Climatically, this region therefore resembles California and the other areas of the globe with a Mediterranean climate. Soils in the winter-rainfall areas of South Africa are diverse, ranging from sands to heavy clays. The latter are often waterlogged during much of the winter, and several species of *Galaxia*, *Spiloxene*, *Gladiolus*, and *Oxalis* commonly spend much of the winter with their stems and underground parts in standing water.

At the University of California Botanical Garden, Berkeley, we have a substantial collection of South African bulbs growing on a gentle southwest-facing slope, where the soil is a heavy clay. Rainfall, all in winter, is about 40 inches, and when temperatures drop into the 20s the foliage of several species shows damage. Our success in growing these plants in the ground has varied — some species (such as *Wachendorfia paniculata* or members of the genus

ROBERT ORNDUFF *is Director of the University of California Botanical Garden, Berkeley, and Professor of Integrative Biology at the university.*

65

RECOMMENDED READING

Bulbous Plants of Southern Africa: A Guide to Their Cultivation and Propagation, by Niel du Plessis and Graham Duncan. 1989, Tafelberg Publishers Ltd., Cape Town.

SOURCES

McCLURE AND ZIMMERMAN
P.O. Box 368
Friesland, WI 53935

AMERICAN PLANT LIFE SOCIETY
P.O. Box 985
National City, CA 92050
(issues annual seed/bulb list with many unusual items

RUST-EN-VREDE NURSERY
P.O. Box 231
7848 Constantia
South Africa

VON LYNCKER NURSERY
P.O. Box 1820
7824 Wynberg
South Africa

HOLMES NURSERY
P.O. Box 6007
7610 Stellenbosch
South Africa

Cyanella) have disappeared due to unknown causes, some grudgingly flower (such as the double form of *Oxalis pes-caprae*) but do not proliferate and others (such as *Gladiolus tristis* and *Babiana* species) have "migrated" out of their sites via seeds and dot the slopes of the garden's African Hill.

Interestingly, one of the worst pests in southern and central California gardens and pastures is the ill-named Bermuda buttercup, *Oxalis pes-caprae*, a beautiful, yellow-flowered South African native that is also pestiferous elsewhere in the world, including South Africa. However, our small colony of this species, collected from a native, non-weedy population in South Africa, is well-behaved, and has stayed put for almost two decades. This species is worth a try, but needs to be watched for potential escapees.

Although the growing season for winter-rainfall South African bulbs is winter, flowering may occur at various times of the year. Once the rains begin in the fall, most *Oxalis* species, as well as some species of *Spiloxene*, *Romulea* and *Lachenalia*, come into flower; the flowers in some may precede the leaves. Other groups flower in mid-season (members of *Watsonia*, *Sparaxis* and *Ornithogalum)*, or late in the season (other species of *Lachenalia* and *Ornithogalum*, and many ground orchids). A few groups flower in the dry season, often long after the leaves have withered. These include the well known *Amaryllis belladonna* and *Nerine* species and hybrids, but also the larger, coarser *Boophone* and *Brunsvigia*. A selection of watsonias can provide flowers from spring through late summer. Favorites of mine are members of the genus *Gethyllis*, which in summer produce fragrant whitish flowers resembling those of *Colchicum*, and if bees are active, a few weeks later the curious, raspberry-scented red fruits emerge from the ground.

Although many South African bulbs (such as *Homeria*) are poisonous and immune to plant-eating pests, gophers can be destructive if they get into bulb beds and can decimate certain choice edibles in a matter of hours. Although moles do not eat bulbs, their burrowing activities can disturb plantings. If moles or gophers are a problem, a raised bed lined with chicken-wire can keep them out. Insect pests seem to be relatively few, although some groups, particularly *Lachenalia*, are susceptible to leaf and stem fungal infections.

Bulbs of most species (except the largest, which you may wish to plant singly) can be planted in small groups of five to two dozen for maximum effect. Species with small bulbs should be planted with the bulb tips one or two inches below the soil surface; larger species can have the bulb tips exposed, and a few (such as the schmoo-like *Boophone*) prosper if the bulbs are placed with just their base touching the soil so that most of the bulb is above ground. This planting practice is not necessary, but the large bulbs sitting on the soil surface add textural interest to the garden.

Although our clay soil suits many species, I think better success would be had if the clay were mixed with coarse sand, or if the bulbs were placed on a sandy substrate two or three inches deep and covered with whatever soil your garden provides. This enhanced drainage might avert some disease problems, but in drier areas it might also mean having to add water during dry spells. Application of a dilute, balanced fertilizer (5-10-10) early in the growing season is often beneficial, though many species do well without this.

Good companion plants are succulents such as *Haworthia*, the smaller aloes and euphorbias, *Gasteria* and many mesembs which thrive under similar conditions. It is probably best to avoid planting your bulbs with drought-tolerant shrubs, as ultimately these shrubs may cast too much shade for the bulbs and also compete for water and nutrients. Placing large rocks throughout the bulb bed can add visual interest as well. Many South African bulbous genera such as *Oxalis* and *Lachenalia* proliferate by producing bulbils, and require lifting and sorting every three or four years, with only the largest bulbs returned to the bed. The smaller "discards" can be traded with a fellow enthusiast. *Lachenalia* can be propagated by leaf cuttings, and many of the larger bulbs can be propagated by shallowly slicing the bulbs. I advise against planting winter-active South African bulbous species where they will receive water in the summer. Some species can tolerate it, but others will rot.

One of the frustrations of attempting to establish a collection of South African bulbs is that so few species are available from dealers in the United States. *Amaryllis belladonna*, *Freesia* hybrids, *Sparaxis*, *Watsonia* and *Ixia*, *Ornithogalum thyrsoides*, a very few *Oxalis* species, *Lachenalia bulbifera* and the Calla "lily" and its relatives, *Zantedeschia*, are not difficult to find at reasonable prices. A few specialty nurseries stock larger numbers of species and genera, many of outstanding horticultural merit, but unfortunately at a *very* high price. My suggestion is that if you locate a domestic source of unusual species, buy what you can afford, start them in pots, and once a small colony has become established via bulbils, try your extras in the ground. Seeds of many unusual species can be obtained from dealers in South Africa, and seedlings of some genera (*Oxalis* and *Lachenalia* are examples) will flower the third year after planting. For beginners, I suggest species of *Homeria, Oxalis, Babiana* (some with wonderfully fragrant flowers), *Watsonia, Sparaxis, Ixia* and *Tritonia*. These all thrive in our heavy clay, and most have survived the severe winters that occur in the Berkeley garden at least once a decade. Fortunately, the South Africans have published a remarkably fine assortment of beautifully illustrated books on their native bulbous plants. It is impossible to describe the variety of floral form, the range of colors, the odd shapes, sizes, spottedness or wartiness of leaves, and the occasional intense fragrance of these plants. The scent of *Freesia* pales compared with the intensity of fragrance of *Gladiolus tenellus*, and a peacock would fold his tail in shame when confronted with the iridescence of *Moraea villosa*. There are many bulbous treasures in South Africa, most of them easy to grow, and in time I hope a wider selection of these will be readily available at moderate prices.

Lachenalia bulbifera.

Romulea tabularis.

Spiloxene capensis.

Sparaxis elegans.

TENDER BULBS FOR SOUTHERN GARDENS

BY EDITH R. EDDLEMAN

Gardens in the middle South need never be without bloom from bulbs. We are fortunate in being able to grow bulbs familiar to Northern gardeners which need winter chilling, such as tulips, narcissus, crocus and snowdrops. Yet our gardens are warm enough for dahlias, crinums, cannas, amaryllis, calla lilies, *Zephyranthes*, gladiolus and elephant ears. Here in central North Carolina (USDA reclassification Zone 7), winter temperatures dip occasionally to 0 degrees F or below, with summer maximum typically 95 to 100 degrees. Average rainfall is about 42 to 45 inches, but summers can be dry.

Crinum

This species has an exotic and tropical look, and combines magnificently in the garden with other plants of tropical appearance. In my own garden, in partial shade, white-flowered crinums grow beside a lovely old bronze-leaved *Canna*. When late afternoon sunlight strikes this planting at an angle, the vein patterns of the canna

EDITH R. EDDLEMAN *is curator and designer of the perennial border at North Carolina State University Arboretum at Raleigh.*

leaves stand out like ruby feathers, a stunning backdrop for the backlit snowy *Crinum* petals. Weaving between these two is a giant fern from central Florida, *Hypolepis repens.*

In general, crinums perform best in moist soils, and I have even seen them planted below the surface in the edge of a pond. However, they are adaptable and do well in my dry sandy soil, flowering from late spring to Thanksgiving, depending on the species. I top dress them with composted manure and leaves in fall. The moment temperatures warm, the foliage starts to grow, so they generally have frost-burned leaf tips. A healthy clump of bulbs may produce foliage five feet across.

From early June through July, *Crinum* 'Cecil Houdyshel' produces a sequence of stalks, each bearing several pale pink, narrow, funnel-shaped flowers. In my garden, the magenta flowers and palmate leaves of *Callirhoe involucrata* spread around its feet. In the Perennial Border at the North Carolina State University Arboretum (NCSUA), this *Crinum* complements the pink, silver and purple mottled foliage of *Berberis thunbergii* 'Rose Glow' and masses of feathery silver *Artemisia* 'Powis Castle'. Elsewhere in the border, it is backed by

Begonia grandis.

the velvety silver-green foliage of pink fall-flowering *Hibiscus grandiflorus*, against a background of 14-foot-tall silver plumed *Miscanthus floridulus*.

The raspberry-pink flaring trumpets of *Crinum* 'Ellen Bosquant' open from deep burnished ruby buds. It is planted in the NCSU border with *Monarda didyma* 'Mahogany' (whose flowers exactly match the *Crinum* bud color), silver-blue flowered *Eryngium alpinum* and moonlight yellow *Achillea taygetea*. In my own garden 'Ellen Bosquant' is surrounded by a taller *Monarda* (whose raspberry-colored blooms exactly match the open flowers of the *Crinum)*, interspersed with rounded blue flower clusters of *Agapanthus praecox* ssp. *orientalis*. These are seen through a magenta haze — the flowers of *Callirhoe digitata* which appear to float in the foreground. The *Agapanthus* are flowering well for the first time since they were planted six years ago. I attribute this to two wet springs in succession — and a top dressing of rotted manure the second spring.

I do not know the name of my favorite milk-and-wine *Crinum*, but resembles *Crinum bulbispermum* and the selection 'Gulf Pride'. It came from a friend's mother's garden in Asheville (in the North Carolina mountains). One of the hardiest crinums I know, this plant survived an overnight dip to -16 degrees F both in Asheville and in Knoxville, Tennessee. The flowers are broad white trumpets with a generous band of soft pink along the keel of each petal. I thought I'd killed a bulb left over winter in a pot. It felt mushy so I composted it. The bulb recovered and grew lustily. It now spends its winters on a Connecticut windowsill.

A bigeneric cross of *Amaryllis belladonna* and *Crinum moorei*, x *Crinodonna*, (formerly x *Amarcrinum howardii*), flowers from late summer through fall. Its arching pleated green leaves and large size — three feet by three feet — recall the *Crinum* parent, while the soft pink, flaring flowers are reminiscent of the *Amaryllis*. In the garden I grow it with *Salvia* x 'Indigo Spires', whose loose flower spikes contrast dramatically with the bold foliage and flowers of x *Crinodonna*. These companions are planted against a backdrop of white-flowered *Lespedeza japonica* and *Boltonia asteroides* 'Pink Beauty'.

Canna

Southern gardeners are lucky enough to be able to leave cannas, elephant ears and

LEFT: *Lycoris radiata* above bracken.
ABOVE: *Lycoris squamigera* and
Phlox paniculata.

dahlias in the ground over the winter. Rich soil and moisture suit cannas to perfection. So grown, they will reward the gardener with lush foliage and lots of flowers. Adaptable cannas also grow in shade, where they make magnificent foliage plants.

RIGHT: *Lycoris squamigera* above the large, glaucous leaves of *Hosta sieboldiana*.

In addition to the old fashioned small-flowered bronze leaved canna, many other cannas claim the attention of garden makers. Sturdy *Canna* 'Wyoming' has broad bronze leaves and glowing orange flowers (described by a colleague as looking like silk handkerchiefs tucked into shirt pockets). Taller, with bronze leaves and small red flowers, is 'King Humbert'. Growing to 14 feet tall, with huge slightly glaucous green leaves and small pale orange blooms, is *Canna* x 'Omega'. It grows in damp soil, combined with gold-banded *Miscanthus sinensis* 'Strictus', huge green *Hosta* 'Pie Crust', elephant ears (*Colocasia esculenta*), the tall fern *Hypolepis repens* and a myriad of other plants in NCSUA border Curator Doug Ruhren's garden.

A handsome new canna, 'Pretoria', has broad green leaves veined in gold, with each leaf outlined in red. Its sturdy stems are purple, topped by flowers the color of apricot jam. While it has been combined in a variety of ways in the garden, my favorite combination is in the garden of the friend, who grows it in front of a golden thread-leaved *Chamaecyparis*, at its feet a late-flowering *Kniphofia* with spiky foliage and orange flowers of the same hue as the canna's. Another canna with green and yellow striped leaves is *C.* 'Nirvana'. It grows three feet tall and has bright yellow flowers which fade in full sun (as does the striping of the leaves).

Planted by the thousands along our roadsides in North Carolina is another fine canna, 'The President'. Masses of these three-foot tall plants with emerald green leaves and large red flowers make a fine summer display. In the NCSUA border, this canna combines well with October-flowering *Helianthus angustifolius*, tall blue *Salvia guaranitica* and the palmate foliage of bronze-leaved castor beans. In general, the large leaves and bright flowers of cannas make a bold statement in the garden. They can be used with great effect with other bold-foliaged plants, or contrasted even more dramatically with fine-textured plants such as ornamental grasses, ferns or the feathery fennel or annual dill.

Ranunculus

The heart-shaped, silver-marbled leaves of the lesser celandine (*Ranunculus ficaria*) come up in winter, carpeting the ground until the end of May. The flowers of the common type are bright yellow, and begin to bloom in February, with the silvery chalices of *Crocus tomasinianus*. *R. ficaria* has a reputation as a garden thug, but so far has shown no such tendencies in my garden. Along the edge of a path, I grow some of the pale forms: 'Randall's White', 'Primrose', 'Albus' and 'Lemon Queen', mixed with a lavender-blue *Phlox divaricatus*, the buttery yellow flowers of *Primula* x *tomasinii*, and the green and white striped foliage of *Disporum sessile* 'Variegatum'. *Ranunculus ficaria* 'Florepleno' has bright yellow double blooms; 'Major' bears large yellow flowers on tall ten inch stems; 'Aurantiacus' has lovely pale orange flowers and particularly silvery green foliage; 'Collarette' is an anemone-centered yellow. 'Greenpetal' features a double row of twisted green sepals instead of petals, its flower reminiscent of the green rose, *Rosa viridiflora*. 'Brazen Hussy' is the name given by Christopher Lloyd to a bronze-leaved form of *R. ficaria* with brilliant lacquer yellow flowers, which he discovered. This form combines well in the garden with the yellow and red striped *Tulipa clusiana* 'Chrysantha' and golden flowered *Aurinia saxatilis*.

Gladiolus

Gladiolus byzantinus is called "Jacob's Ladder" by some Southern gardeners. The bright glow of its magenta flowers often signals the location of old home sites. I have seen this species growing in old farm fields.

Eucomis bicolor.

Its tall flower sprays are produced in April above fans of dark green foliage. Suitable companions are pink and white early-flowering *Verbena canadensis* and lavender and white *Verbena tenuisecta* and *Phlox pilosa*.

Hippeastrum (Amaryllis)

The large-flowered or "Dutch" *Hippeastrum Amaryllis* hybrids usually grown as pot plants seem perfectly hardy in our climate. I plant the large bulbs just below the soil surface. A fall top dressing of organic matter encourages good flowering the following spring. Flowers appear before the straplike leaves emerge. One of the delights of the Perennial Border in spring is the striking red-orange trumpets of the cultivar 'Basutoland', flowering with bronze-foliaged dahlias and white *Achillea millefolium. Hippeastrum* x *johnsoni* is commonly grown in the open a bit farther south. Someone kindly provided me with three bulbs, which spent the winter in a pot on my windowsill. The flowers are tomato red with a distinctive white star in the center.

Hippeastrum advenum is a delightful fall-blooming amaryllid sold variously as *Amaryllis advena, Rhodophiala advena*. In North Carolina, it is known as the oxblood lily, so called for its narrow, red, trumpet-shaped flowers. German settlers brought it to Texas, where it is called the schoolhouse lily, because it blooms at the start of fall classes. Shiny green leaves follow the flowers, and remain green throughout winter. This bulb is planted in a sandy, sunny spot in my garden. In the lath house of the NCSU Arboretum, it grows in part shade in a raised bed of fine pine bark and gravel to which lime and fertilizer have been added. In six years, a single bulb has become a generous clump. The bold green leaves and fragrant flowers of the August lily *Hosta plantaginea* make a suitable background.

Elizabeth Lawrence liked to grow *Hippeastrum advenum* with the lacy foliage and white flowers of *Asteromoea mongolica* and *Verbena tenuisecta* 'Alba'. In the border dedicated to her at the NCSU Arboretum, the oxblood lily blooms in the shade of *Polygonatum cuspidatum* (which produces feathery sprays of red-bracted flowers at the same time), above a carpet of silvery leaved purple *Sedum* 'Vera Jameson' and purple-leaved *Heuchera* 'Palace Purple'.

Dahlia

Dahlias, bred from plants native to Mexico, do not have to be lifted for the winter in the

ABOVE: *Alstroemeria psittacina.* **AT RIGHT:** *Ipheion uniflorum.*

South. The tuberous roots can be planted fairly deep (six to eight inches) to protect them from winter cold. Dahlias are heavy feeders, growing well in soils with a high organic content. A top dressing of composted manure works well. Regular watering produces the best flowering. One notable selection in the NCSU Perennial Border is the cactus-flowered, light pink *Dahlia* 'Park Princess', two feet tall, planted with *Aster frikartii*, *Salvia leucantha* and a silvery ground cover of *Potentilla villosa*. In the hot-colored part of my garden, *Dahlia* 'Bishop of Llandaff', with semi-double orange-red flowers and bronze foliage, complements *Hemerocallis* 'Stella d'Oro', *Salvia coccinea*, *Salvia superba* 'May Night', the pink and cream foliage of *Hypericum moserianum* 'Tricolor', bronze fennel, the scarlet and orange flowers of

annual tasselflower (*Emilia javanica*) and gold-banded *Miscanthus sinensis* 'Strictus'.

Eucomis

The pineapple lilies *Eucomis bicolor* and *E. punctata* are exotic in appearance. Broad clumps of leaves give rise to sturdy stems which carry flowers topped with another set of leaves resembling little pineapples. *E. bicolor* generally has green leaves and white flowers, while the foliage of *E. punctata* may be purplish, and the flowers tinted pink. Even a single *Eucomis* makes a striking accent.

Alstroemeria

Parrot lily is the common name for the curious *Alstroemeria psittacina*. Tall stems clothed in whorls of green leaves bear clusters of red-and-green blossoms in early summer. After the flowers fade, elegant seed pods develop. The foliage is evergreen in winter. It prefers partial shade, and its flowers show to advantage against the cream and green variegated foliage of *Euonymus* 'Silver King'. The further south one travels, the weedier this plant is inclined to be.

Arum

I started my horticultural career as a windowsill gardener and greenhouse grower of tropical plants. The first plant to draw me out into the garden was *Arum italicum* (formerly *A. italicum* 'Pictum'), which I saw growing in a raised bed covered with ivy beneath a huge maple in my great-aunt Edith's garden. The bed and the arum had been there for over 60 years. The large arrowhead-shaped leaves marbled in cream enchanted me. They remained through the winter, and when the spring brought the pale-green spathes, I was even more impressed. The spathes were followed by a green seeds on the spadix, which ripened to orange by late summer. The arums do not like sandy soil, so try planting the tubers in a rich compost mixture. Given good soil and moisture, *Arum italicum* will grow well in either sun or shade.

Elephant Ears

Elephant ears (*Colocasia esculenta*) were favorites in Victorian gardens. Their heart-shaped leaves, reaching two to three feet (or more) in length, on stems up to eight feet tall, have a decidedly tropical appearance. However, here in central North Carolina, they can remain in the ground through the winter. Colocasias grow best in soils rich in organic matter (rotted leaves and manure) kept constantly moist. Elephant ears may be grown in full sun to full shade. Ferns, *Hosta*, cannas, callas, *Crinum* and large ornamental grasses are good companions.

Zantedeschia

Calla lilies (which are not true lilies) do well in Southern gardens. *Zantedeschia aethiopica*, the white calla, is common. It has dark green leaves (sometimes spotted with white) and pure white flowers. *Z. elliottiana* has beautiful arrow-shaped leaves heavily spotted with silver, and butter yellow spathes. It flowers from late spring through early summer. *Zantedeschia rehmannii* gives rise to pink and burgundy spathed selections. The leaves are narrow compared to the above species, and often solid green.

Callas flower well in soils that are moist or well-watered, performing well in sun or in shade. Like elephant ears, they can overwinter in our climate without being lifted.

Ipheion

Ipheion uniflorum, the garlic-scented blue

Zantedeschia aethiopica.

star flower, carpets Southern lawns in spring. Its delicately blue-tinted flowers are veined with purple. The low gray-green foliage dies down quickly after the flowers fade. The selection 'Wisley Blue' has deeper blue flowers, which are the perfect foil to the glaucous broad needle-tipped foliage and chartreuse flowers of *Euphorbia myrsinites*. The English cultivar 'Froye Mill' bears violet colored flowers. A friend of mine has found a form with large pristine white flowers growing in a Virginia lawn.

Zephyranthes

Atamasco lilies (*Zephyranthes*) occur in moist meadows throughout North Carolina. In the western part of the state, they are known by their Indian name "Cullowhee." In spring, pink-tinted buds open to upward-facing white trumpets touched with pink. When my mother was a little girl, she transplanted an Atamasco lily, *Zephyranthes atamasco*, into her mother's garden. It grew and bloomed for several years, then vanished. One spring day thirty years later, as Mother was walking in the garden, she saw the Atamasco lily in bloom once more, in the spot where she had planted it. Despite their preference for moist soils, these bulbs have done well in my sandy soils enriched with compost, where they bloom in spring amid masses of mauve-pink *Phlox pilosa* 'Ozarkiana' and lavender-blue *Phlox divaricata*.

Blooming in August and September is the white-flowered *Zephyranthes candida*. Buds are produced from clumps of narrow evergreen foliage. I came across a dramatic planting as I was driving along the back roads of piedmont North Carolina. Thousands of these bulbs lined a formal walk sweeping from the street to the front door of a large Georgian residence. Viewing this sheet of silver I was reminded that the La Plata river of Argentina gets its name ("the silver river") from the profusion of these small bulbs which line its banks.

Lycoris

In July, gardens are enlivened by the soft pink, flaring trumpets of *Lycoris squamigera*. Its common names, "naked ladies" and "magic lilies," refer to the fact that the scape appears without foliage. (A clump of gray-green broad leaves appears each winter and dies down before summer.) The scapes rise elegantly above the foliage of blue-leaved hostas, or with Japanese painted fern (*Athyrium nippon-*

icum). I love to see their flowers among blue *Agapanthus*, pink and white phlox and the rose-red *Monarda* 'Adam'. This species is remarkably cold hardy. A group of bulbs barely rooted in soil have survived above-ground in my garden for five years.

Less cold hardy is *Lycoris radiata*, known in the South as "spider lily" because of its long, spidery anthers which emerge from the throats of its red flowers. Like its pink cousin*s*, this species flowers (in September) before foliage appears. Tufts of narrow dark-green leaves with a white midrib emerge in winter. The scapes of *L. radiata* look lovely above the filigreed green foliage of *Selaginella involvens*. My grandmother grew red spider lilies at the base of *Nandina domestica*, underplanted with *Vinca minor*. The color of the flowers reflected the red and rust shades in the *Nandina* foliage. At NCSU, *Lycoris radiata*

LEFT: *Hippeastrum advenum.*

BELOW LEFT: *Crinum* sp.

BELOW: *Hedychium coronarium.*

ABOVE RIGHT: *Arum italicum.*

BELOW RIGHT: *Lycoris radiata.*

is planted among clumps of the red-tipped Japanese bloodgrass, *Imperata cylindrica* 'Red Baron'.

Allium

The showy flowers of *Allium* can add interest to any garden. In May the silvery lavender heads of chives (*Allium schoenoprasum*) rise above rounded clumps of edible green foliage, splendid beside the flowers of lavender moss verbena (*Verbena tenuisecta*) and pink *Phlox pilosa*. Bloom continues for about a month. A pink-flowered form of chives (*A. schoenoprasum* 'Forescate') is an excellent companion to *Geranium* 'Russell Pritchard'.

Many showy *Allium* flourish only in Mediterranean climates. One of the best-adapted for North Carolina is *A. sphaerocephalum*, the drumstick allium. Native to Great Britain and Europe, it likes our summer moisture. The foliage reminds me of wild garlic — I have to be careful not to weed these bulbs in spring. A well developed clump produces many oval clusters of red-violet flowers on three-foot stems fom late May through June. In a planting with the creamy-pink *Hemerocallis* 'Better Believe It', the red-violet eye of the daylily is enhanced by the similarly colored flowers of the drumstick allium. Or one can plant *A. sphaerocephalum* with silver-leaved *Artemisia* and pink phlox.

Allium flavum flowers in July in North Carolina. The gray-green cylindrical foliage is eight to ten inches high. Clusters of soft-yellow pendulous flowers on 12 foot stems appear for several weeks. Suitable companions are the ground-hugging bronze leaved *Veronica* 'Waterperry', golden marjoram, and purple-leaved *Perilla frutescens* 'Crispa'.

Allium tuberosum, garlic chives, produces clumps of flat-sided flavorful leaves.

From late summer to fall, starry white flower clusters are borne above the foliage on 18-inch stems. These combine well in the garden with late-flowering daylilies, *Gaillardia*, red and purple verbenas and *Sedum* x 'Autumn Joy'.

Allium stellatum, native to the central and eastern U.S., adds a touch of elegance to fall gardens., Its rose-pink flowers are carried on foot-high stems. Plant this species behind the silvery lavender leaves of *Sedum* 'Vera Jameson', in front of pink-flowered *Abelia* x 'Edward Goucher'. *Allium thunbergii* 'Osaka's Form' is less than a foot tall, and flowers in October. The flowers are a deep violet.

Habranthus

"Copper lilies" is an apt name for *Habranthus texanus*. Its slender stem, six to eight inches tall, carries a small, upward-facing flower whose petals are a coppery red-brown on the outside. Inside, the flower is yellow flushed with orange. These plants set seed rapidly; the seeds look like slivers of charcoal.

Begonia

Native to China, *Begonia grandis* is tuberous. From late August through September, sprays of pink flowers (white in the form 'Alba') are produced on two-inch-tall plants — except in my dry sandy garden where the plants are one foot tall. The succulent stems flushed with red at the nodes, and red-haired leaves shaped like angel wings, make this a striking plant even when not in flower. In the South, a fair amount of shade is necessary to the continued well-being of these plants, as they crisp up in the sun. This begonia is an ideal companion for ferns, hostas and *Tricyrtis*. A striking combination is the white-flowered form of *B. grandis* and the deep violet flowers of *Tri-*

Habranthus texanus.

cyrtis hirta 'Sinnome'. The pink-flowered form of this begonia is lovely with the fuzzy blue flowers of *Eupatorium coelestinum*. The bulbils produced at each leaf node can be collected and planted wherever another clump of this fresh autumn flower is desired.

Hedychium

The ginger lily, *Hedychium coronarium*, produces satiny white flowers with a spicy fragrance in the fall. The foliage resembles a dainty canna, and like the canna, the ginger lily grows from a rhizome. Stems four to six feet tall are clothed in medium-green leaves that taper to a point. I have always grown *Hedychium* in full sun. An evergreen hedge behind it seems to give it all the protection it needs. A friend who grows it in her country garden covers the rhizomes with boughs of cedar. It may need more cover farther south. Although reputed to prefer rich soil and frequent watering, *H. coronarium* has been amenable to fairly dry conditions. Like most of the "bulbs" mentioned in this article, ginger lilies benefit from a fall mulch of rich organic matter.

Nerine

Hardiest of the nerines, *Nerine bowdenii* is native to the Cape Province of South Africa. These flower in piedmont North Carolina in late October. Loose umbels of silver pink or hot pink flowers are carried on 15-inch stems. My bulbs put up foliage in summer, before the flowers appear. This *Nerine* makes a valiant attempt to remain evergreen throughout the winter, but its leaves generally freeze to the ground in our climate. I grow the bright pink form against a gray-blue/lavender and silver background planting of *Buddleia* 'Lochinch' and *Aster* x *frikartii* 'Wonder of Staffa'. A pale pink form grows in front of a *Callicarpa americana*. A pale pink *Aster caroliniana* scrambles through the branches of the *Callicarpa*. A sunny, well drained and protected winter location helps *Nerine bowdenii* foliage to ripen and mature.

Schizostylis

Schizostylis coccinea looks like a dainty gladiolus. Sprays of buds open in October to November, producing rounded satiny red flowers. In its native habitat, this plant grows in wet places, often with its roots in water. It therefore appreciates frequent watering, particularly during the month before it blooms, and during the flowering

83

period. The cultivar 'Sunrise' has pink flowers; those of 'Viscountess Byng' are a paler pink. Flowers of 'Oregon Sunset' are a coppery color. *Schizostylis* spreads by a thin white rhizomatous rootstock and multiplies fairly quickly.

Southern gardeners who wish to venture beyond the realm of the ordinary need not limit their bulb plantings to these selections. Additional options include such exotics as *Tulbaghia violacea* ("society garlic"), *Crocosmia* (sometimes called *Montbretia*), many species of *Oxalis* and a multitude of other plants which must move indoors during winter farther north.

Many of the bulbs discussed here can be ordered from traditional bulb suppliers or nurseries. Greenhouse catalogs also advertise as house plants a surprising number of bulbs which can overwinter outdoors in Zone 7 and above.

Crinum sp.

CROCUS, NARCISSUS, TULIPS AND LILIES FOR SOUTHERN GARDENS

BY EDITH R. EDDLEMAN

Crocus

In the mid South, crocus begin and end the year. But our extended fall season makes the autumn and early winter crocus particularly delightful.

Unlike most commonly grown crocuses, *Crocus goulymyii* produces foliage and flowers at the same time. Clusters of lavender-pink blooms emerge from the grassy clumps of leaves from September into October. This species was discovered in 1954 in the Balkans by Dr. Goulym, for whom it was named. I planted bulbs of this crocus with divisions of a mauve-pink *Verbena tenuisecta* seedling which occurred by chance in my garden. The lacy foliage of the verbena provides textural contrast, while the color of its flowers repeats that of the crocus.

October brings the blossoms of *Crocus medius*. Its deep blue-violet flowers are set off by fiery orange anthers. Their color is attractive against the silvery winter leaf rosettes of *Lychnis coronaria*.

Elizabeth Lawrence called *Crocus ochroleucus* "a poor wraith," but it always reminds me of glistening pearly drops pushing up out of the cold November soil. In a good year it flowers from mid-November into December. In my garden it is interspersed with spring-flowering *C. chrysanthus* 'Cream Beauty' beneath a large crape myrtle (*Lagerstroemia indica*). I love to see the yellow-throated white flowers with the pale cream and beige mottled bark of the tree.

December is ushered in by the silver-lilac goblets of *Crocus laevigatus* var. *fontenayi*. The three outer perianth segments of each flower are feathered with deep violet. In a cold icy December, the flower buds hunker down and wait for warmer weather, and may flower all through January. I purchased my bulbs listed as *C. laevigatus* var. *fontaneyi*, but Brian Mathew in *The Crocus* indicates that the varietal name has no botanical validity and should be omitted.

Narcissus

Depending on where one starts, the first or last narcissus to bloom in my garden is the small hybrid hoop-petticoat known as 'Nylon', who usually shakes out her skirts around the eighth of December. In my garden grow several 'Nylon' clones, descended from a batch of seedlings produced in a single cross made by Donald Blanchard. All of the clones I've grown are alike in the pale lemon translucent quality of their petals which quickly fade to a soft cream color. I grow these small narcissus in well drained soil at the south-facing edge of a stone terrace, where the bulbs are allowed to bake in the summer.

When I was a child, the first daffodils of spring in our garden were *Narcissus pseudonarcissus*. We called them "Jonquils," a term many Southerners use to designate all members of the genus *Narcissus*. Usually blooming in February, this species will occasionally unfurl its buds in January if the winter is unusually warm. The foliage is short, blunt-tipped and green. The butter-yellow trumpets are surrounded by paper-thin creamy petals. Some years, the blooms of these *Narcissus* overlap with the dainty blue arching flower sprays of Roman hyacinths (*Hyacinthus orientalis* v. *albulus*).

Dearest to me of all the old narcissus grown in southern gardens is the swan's neck daffodil, *Narcissus moschatus*. The broad foliage of this daffodil is a glaucous gray-green in color. The creamy white flower is borne on a 12 to 15 inch stem in early spring. Its petals droop forward toward the long trumpet-shaped cup. My precious bulb came from a garden in Hillsborough, North Carolina, where this variety was growing when a friend and her husband bought the property many years ago. The swan's neck daffodil is not common in commerce, being in my experience slow to increase, but it can often be found in old Southern gardens. My own bulb (now grown to two after four years) is planted in a bed which is quite shaded in summer (though sunny in spring) and dry. Planted near the swan's neck are *Muscari*, the cheerful "blue bottles" of southern gardens. This year I've decided to add to this blue-and-silver color scheme a carpet of blue *Anemone blanda*.

"Campernells" is the common name for *Narcissus* x *odorus*. Early in spring, tall stems carry several fragrant yellow single flowers above green foliage that resembles knitting needles. *Narcissus* x *odorus* var. *plenus* has double flowers. This fragrant early-blooming daffodil inhabits old Southern gardens. This spring, after many an attempt to acquire it through mail order firms (who always supplied the wrong bulb), I found a row of them growing alongside a narrow dirt road in the country. I leapt from my car, and knocked on the door of the farmhouse. No one was home, but I left a note asking if the owner might like to sell a few daffodils. Happily, the owner called, and now a clump of these precious bulbs resides in my own garden.

"Pheasant-eye" was our name for *Narcissus poeticus* v. *recurvus*, with broad blue-green foliage and tall stems, each bearing a white flower with a short yellow cup rimmed in red. These are planted in my garden beneath a hybrid serviceberry,

Anemone blanda.

Amelanchier x *grandiflora* (which flowers heavily every other year), and in front of evergreen *Helleborus foetidus*, with green bell-shaped flowers lipped in red, repeating the red-outlined eye of the *Narcissus*.

"Twin sisters" is the charming Southern name for *Narcissus* x *medioluteus* (formerly *N. biflorus*). Twin flowers with creamy white petals and short soft yellow cups are borne at the tip of 18 inch stems, above soft gray-green clumps of leaves. In general,

this is the final narcissus of spring, flowering in late April or early May.

Tulips

Southern gardeners are not used to thinking of tulips as permanent residents of the garden, though some old cultivars do persist here. The two tulips which are most successful in my own garden are *Tulipa batalinii* and *T. clusiana*. *T. batalinii* is eight inches tall with pale butter-yellow

Crocus ochroleucus.

Crocus goulymii.

flowers and blue-green recurved leaves with red edges. In a friend's rock garden, I saw it growing amidst clouds of blue phlox, with candytuft *(Iberis sempervirens)*, *Anemonella thalictroides*, the foamy white spires of *Tiarella cordifolia* and blue scillas.

The flowers of the lady tulip, *Tulipa clusiana*, are red and white striped like peppermints. (The variety 'Chrysantha' with red and yellow stripes is equally successful.) The 16 inch stems of the lady tulip always look a little lost in my garden, so I offer a planting suggestion from Elizabeth Lawrence, who liked to grow a mass of them edged by clumps of red and white flowered English daisies (*Bellis perennis*), which can be bought as bedding plants in late fall or early spring. White *Oxalis crassipes* would also be an elegant companion.

Lilium

When I started gardening, I was not sure that lilies could be grown in Southern gardens because I had never seen them in my aunt's or grandmother's gardens. Looking back, I believe lilies weren't grown because my relatives gardened in extremely heavy clay soils. I grow many cultivars in the North Carolina State University Arboretum Perennial Border. A part of the secret of their success is planting the bulb tilted at an angle, so that water drains away from the scales. My favorite lilies are the Asian species and hybrids of *Lilium speciossimum*. In the 50 percent shade of our lath house and its loose bark planting beds, these bulbs quickly naturalized among the ferns. The sight of hundreds of pink red-freckled lilies nodding above the lacy foliage of the ferns is one I'll never forget. I have also grown this lily in full sun and regular garden soil.

Lilium formosum grows six to eight inches tall, carrying slender cream-white trumpets above stems clothed in whorls of drooping green leaves. The dried seed pods of this species are lovely in flower arrangements. Easily grown from seed, flowering plants can be produced from an early spring sowing. Compact forms of *L. formosum* are offered by at least one nursery.

A Final Note

This is only a sampling of the crocuses, narcissus, lilies, and tulips available to the mid-South gardener. Remember that virtually all of these bulbs (not just the lilies) require good drainage. And many of these bulbs are species rather than varieties. Some may be endangered in their natural habitat. When ordering bulbs, make sure that they are nursery propagated and not collected from the wild.

Lilium speciosum.

THE DRAMA OF BULBS

BY HARLAND J. HAND

Fritillaria imperialis.

The emotional charge that I got as a child from seeing the first leaves of tulips and the lifting little white flower bells of snowdrops in the long-awaited Minnesota spring has never been equaled in all my experiences with plants. As a result I remain charged every time I look at a flowering bulb, especially those of early spring.

Bulbs usually flash their colors, follow with a modest but nourishing growth cycle, then bow out completely for a long rest.

Because their annual appearances are so abrupt, it is hard to best them for drama. Each new flowering is like the unexpected discovery of long forgotten jewels.

Some bulbs proliferate in my garden. What a delightful surprise to find them in wonderfully unexpected relationships as they spread about or as other plants encroach. And some bulbs are forgotten, overcome by their neighbors or having naturalized into some unwanted relationship.

Many garden-variety bulbs, like most modern garden plants, have become so selected and hybridized that they hardly resemble their original parents. Fortu-

HARLAND J. HAND *is an artist who lives and gardens in El Cerrito, California.*

Crinum.

nately, some still have at least the feel of their ancestors, so I often go to those ancestors and to their natural habitats to find the special details that can make the "inspired design."

I garden in the San Francisco Bay Area, where summers are dry and winters are wet and usually frost free — very different from the rest of the continent. Because I am an artist, I enjoy solving the resulting garden design problems. I look at all kinds of plant groupings (bulbs included), especially in the wilderness, to find inspiration and solutions (but never to copy). For this reason, I am not greatly bothered that in my garden snowdrops last only a year or two, and tulips repeat only if they are away from the sprinklers and allowed to stay dry during summer. *Fritillaria imperialis* will not even break dormancy after the mild winter in my area. However, I find numerous bulbs that do wonderfully well here.

Daffodil blooming among azaleas.

Many small, low-growing bulbs flourish in my garden. Seeing them, I think of soaring alpine meadows, rugged rocky outcrops and other places where plants appear either to thrive or struggle, hugging the surfaces so they do not blow or fall away. Creviced granite, grassy hillsides, the sparse scree of mountain and desert or wherever small bulbs naturalize are habitats that inspire me. I have clumps of pink rain lilies (*Zephyranthes grandiflora*) blooming intermittently and unexpectedly in summer, a few at a time, in crevices (the crevices in my garden are two to four inch spaces between the elliptical concrete slabs that, along with coarse gravel, cover the flat areas of my garden). Through a sprawling line of Reiter's thyme, a clump of *Triteleia uniflora* rises horizontally and just tall enough for a show of starry lavender on a bed of the thyme's deep green. The long sprawling leaves of *Muscari armeniacum* grow throughout the year in my garden; their flowers appear intermittently, a few at a time, but in March they turn the crevices blue with bunches of tiny blue-violet balloons atop six inch stems — that was, before my plague of gophers. Petticoat daffodils (*Narcissus bulbocodium*) play drifting games across the garden where the gophers (they don't eat daffodils) have carried them, always to an interesting place (so far). Recently I discovered that I can thwart gophers by building little concrete barriers across the crevices. They are hidden just beneath the surface of the soil, thick and deep enough to block (or redirect) the tunneling that would lead in a direct line from one succulent morsel to another.

Sometimes muscari, petticoat daffodils and the fragrant freesias grow so profusely that they become most pleasant pests. What a puzzling pleasure to decide which ones to leave and which to remove. A really nice thing about prolific small bulbs is that they can also be used in clumps at the edge of the level areas and at the bases of rocks, small shrubs and perennials, where they form a colorful transitional anchor each spring. This way they also add to the flowing form of my hillside garden, enhancing the naturalistic scene without hiding rocks or other low plants.

Some bulbs thrive under small stones. *Cyclamen persicum* naturalizes by seeding into the coarse gravel. It is touching to see their delicate large pink flowers (the only color that seems to proliferate) force the pebbles aside and take their positions here and there across such ruggedly textured places. The contrast of meek delicacy and rugged strength is always deeply moving.

I am experimenting with the lachenalias. *Lachenalia aloides* (yellow with orange tip) forms large clumps in the crevices, especially if they are kept on the dry side in summer. I am hoping that other species new to me will become good partners for the muscari.

Standing taller than the ground huggers, bulbs such as daffodils, *Sparaxis* and the shorter lilies, when planted close by the taller shrubs and perennials, seem to visually anchor them to the ground. Most shrubs will grow out and over these "anchors" if they are not kept pruned. This can be a disaster if the bulbs are overwhelmed. But flowers peeking out through a shrub are always an amusing surprise. I find that daffodils and some other narcissus will continue in this position indefinitely — neither dying out nor proliferating. My *Sparaxis tricolor* thrive sprawling out from under the edge of shrubs, with their shallow-growing bulbs safely secluded. Their white-centered yellow flowers (other colors are available) foam out in masses — "flowing" everything together as they float down banks and over rocks. Their masses of flowers bloom for weeks.

Growing between, under and through shrubs or tall perennials is what the tallest lilies seem to especially like. Auratums, regals and rubrums will thrive for years growing through shrubs, their feet in the shade and their flowers exposed above for all — bees, hummingbirds and humans — to see. In the wilds of Mount Shasta, the pale gray-flowered native *Lilium washingtonianum* thrives doing just that. *Lilium parvum* and its wild varieties will grow to huge clumps in the company of our native azalea (*Rhododendron occidentalis*) and other shrubs. In the garden, lilies must be fed early in their growing season wherever they are grown with shrubs. Shrubs that share the food must be pruned annually so as not to overwhelm their bulbous companions.

Because they are bulbs of the grassland, especially the Midwestern prairies, turk's cap and many umbel types of lilies usually grow about knee-high. In nature, they bloom when their companion grasses are in flower and they enjoy the partial shade of swaying, wind-blown prairie plants. However, asters and closed gentians grow taller and soon hide the developing seed pods, expanding bulbs and palling leaves of the lilies. Species of goldenrod, *Rudbeckia* and other perennials will grow to over six feet in the climactic color carnival of late summer and fall; by that time the lilies have retired for their annual rest. All the Midwestern prairie growth will be leveled by winter winds and snow. With spring, birds-foot violets and low bulbs start the entire floral display all over again. I grow many of the "knee-high" lilies with low perennials (such as violets), taller perennials (asters and various daisies) and grasses, including oat grass and clumps of *Festuca*. Someday I would like to experiment with the whole prairie flower sequence.

In the wild, many bulbous plants grow in open spaces within a forest, or at its edge; erythroniums are among the loveliest. Knowing this, I am comfortable placing flowering bulbs near taller shrubs and trees. I also see many bulbous plants growing among the wildflowers and tall grasses of rural fence rows. Since fence rows are a naturalized part of a farm (the farm is the original source of most Western garden ideas), this could very well be where the idea of borders, especially the perennial border, originated. However, the naturalized fence row and the forest edge seem much more earthy, exciting and profound than the traditional, super-refined perennial border.

The thin vertical *Ixia* and the nodding, heavy-bud-tipped *Dierama* inflorescences sway in every breeze. I grow these corms in clumps among succulents, geraniums, low growing perennials and shrubs. Since they behave like grassland plants, I am now trying them among grasses. Occasionally I allow them to grow in crevices for a temporary touch of swaying, wind-wand movement over a flat area, but never in numbers that become a barrier to either eye or foot. Both ixias and dierama are "see through" plants; that is, they have such thin towering lines that the garden beyond them can still be seen — a wonderfully "moving" effect on gently breezy days. The newer ixias (in deep bright pinks and rich reds, or white with surprising touches of blue-green from the rare species *Ixia viridiflora*) are usually very vigorous and grow as tall as dieramas and gladiolus.

Crinums and other bulbs with heavy

flowers and massive foliage perform dramatically as silhouettes against dark shrubs or against an expanse of light sun-drenched color. These plants can be like sculptures in a sculpture garden, except, being plants, they appear quite at home in most gardens.

I don't always fertilize bulbs, but I do (usually in early spring) if they have shown weakening growth and always when they show fewer flowers. I also move bulbs; when they crowd each other, when they are being overcome by other plants or whenever they have ceased responding well to their garden situation.

When the bulbs begin to go dormant, the garden can seem tired and poorly groomed. The leaves turn from green to yellow to sun-bleached tan. So, where the bulb "debris" is not concealed by other plants, I try to "design in" this season to create a scene of contrasting drama. If the garden has enough dark and light color contrast or enough textures and colors that complement the color of the retiring growth, it will seem a purposeful drama of slumber and wakefulness — instead of a bothersome mess.

Echeveria elegans with *Sparaxis grandiflora* at right.